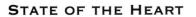

STATE OF THE HEART

State of the Heart

*South Carolina Writers on
the Places They Love*

EDITED BY AÏDA ROGERS

FOREWORD BY PAT CONROY

THE UNIVERSITY OF SOUTH CAROLINA PRESS

© 2013 University of South Carolina

Published by the University of South Carolina Press
Columbia, South Carolina 29208

www.sc.edu/uscpress

Manufactured in the United States of America

22 21 20 19 18 17 16 15 14 13   10 9 8 7 6 5 4 3 2 1

Library of Congress Cataloging-in-Publication Data
State of the heart : South Carolina writers on the places they love /
[edited by] Aida Rogers ; [foreword by] Pat Conroy.
     pages cm
   ISBN 978-1-61117-250-8 (hardback) — ISBN 978-1-61117-251-5
(paperback) — ISBN 978-1-61117-252-2 (epub) 1. South Carolina—
Literary collections. 2. American literature—21st century. I. Rogers,
Aida. editor of compilation.
   PS558.S6S73 2013
   810.8'0358757—dc23

                                   2012045550

This book was printed on a recycled paper with 30 percent
postconsumer waste content.

He said had Al Hafed remained at home and dug in his own cellar or in his own garden, instead of wretchedness, starvation, poverty, and death— a strange land, he would have had "acres of diamonds"—for every acre, yes, every shovelful of that old farm afterwards revealed the gems which since have decorated the crowns of monarchs.

Russell H. Conwell

CONTENTS

☽ *Evening Quiet*

ILLUSTRATIONS

FOREWORD *State of Surprise*

South Carolina is a state of constant surprise and ceaseless story. When I arrived in state in 1961, I learned to fully expect the unconventional, the unusual, and always the great surprising thing. There was an albino porpoise swimming in the Harbor River the first time I drove out to visit the glorious beach on Hunting Island. When I filled up with a tank of gas in Columbia, I became eligible for a free car wash and given a handful of chicken necks to feed to a live Bengal tiger who attracted many customers, especially the children of South Carolina. An eighteen-foot alligator washed up dead on Fripp Island, and I once saw hundreds of thousands of horseshoe crabs mating during a full moon out on Land's End in the Broad River.

In the spring our rivers fill up with migrating fish moving into freshwater rivers and creeks to lay their eggs according to the primal urges of heredity. The shad surrender egg sacs that gourmet restaurants prize as one of the great delicacies of the sea and huge cobia provide steaks for the grills of lowcountry people. Men and women throw their cast-nets with gestures of infinite beauty, and they can fill their freezers with shrimp for a half season on a good night. The osprey dive for mullet in golf-course lagoons and chase bald eagles away from their nests. Nature is everywhere in South Carolina and there is no escape from it or any reason to do so. There are herds of whitetail deer roaming the forests and swamps throughout the state and 600-pound feral hogs are endangering farmland around the Edisto. There are sharks that can kill you swimming in Charleston Harbor and water moccasins that can kill you in the blackwater creeks along the Ashepoo. The oysters of the May River are as delicious as the Belons sold in Paris restaurants and the rainbow trout pulled up by fly fishermen on the Chattooga are as pretty as tarot cards.

Then there are the people of South Carolina. As a novelist, I felt as lucky to have come to South Carolina as a fifteen-year-old boy as any writer that ever lived. I couldn't be happier or more grateful if I'd been born on the family estate of Leo Tolstoy, Yasnaya Polyana. This green, river-shaped state abounds with stories that are full of raw humor and startling intimacy. There are tellers of tall tales who can dominate a room with their mastery of the form. When I met Alex Sanders, the former appellate chief judge and president of the College of Charleston, he delivered a cornucopia of magical, perfectly wrought stories that I've purloined for my own novels in the last forty years. At Beaufort High School, I met the madcap, over-caffeinated Bernie Schein who would keep me in stitches for the rest of my life. Ernest Hollings elbowed me out of the way in a whirlpool at the Citadel and said, "Get out of my way, cadet. Your Governor needs to soak his leg." He entertained me with bizarre, but vivid stories of politics in my new state. Strom Thurmond sat beside my brother Jim on the statehouse steps when Jim was in college. At first the Senator was quiet, then looked at Jim and said, "Son, eating asparagus always makes your urine stink."

The subject of food is a serious one the length and breadth of this state. Our barbeque sauce is mustard-based and our peanuts are boiled and served in wet paper bags. An oyster roast in sight of a lowcountry river is an act of priest-like enjoyment and cause for a pagan-like joy. At a Charleston hospital during my Citadel years, I met a leper who told me he contracted leprosy when he killed and ate an armadillo. I've no idea if he was telling the truth or not, but I didn't wish to shake his hand and armadillo meat shall never pass my lips—but that's the kind of thing that turns up when you're moseying around South Carolina and you don't mind talking to strangers.

The habits of the natives are catchable and permanent. The Clemson-Carolina game is a Eucharistic, God-haunted event that is treated as a moveable feast in the South Carolina calendar year. I've been to several of these primitive, Cro-Magnon events where animals were slaughtered by the thousands and the smell of meat sizzling on charcoal grills outside of huge amphitheaters causes orgasmic excitement all over the state. By accident, I stumbled into this realm of controversy. When I wrote *The Prince of Tides*, I knew I wanted to include a Clemson-Carolina game in which my protagonist, Tom Wingo, would run back a punt and a kickoff to win the game for Clemson. I thought Tommy Wingo, the son of a shrimper, would be likelier to attend Clemson on a football scholarship than to attend the tonier University of South Carolina. Such language could get one killed in this state.

My taciturn and grouchy brothers all checked in with me after my father betrayed me by letting on that I'd granted Clemson a victory in my newest book. Mike, Jim, Tim, and Tom had all attended USC and were fierce in their uncommon devotion to their alma mater and their utter contempt for Clemson. They threatened never to buy the book, read the book, recommend the book, or have it brought into their homes, because they had such a traitor for a brother.

In an act of complete literary cowardice, I went back to the offending chapter and every time I said "Clemson," I wrote down "South Carolina," and then reversed the process until my brothers' school won the annual contest gone awry. I had pacified my brothers, but never appeased them. Our family had changed forever when we moved to Beaufort so many years ago. It's an easy state to love and a hard one to leave.

But, on occasion, South Carolina can rise up and steal your soul with a moment so magical it seems like an exorcism. It has happened to me dozens of times since I've taken up residence here. The sight of the sun setting in all its gold-rimmed majesty over a great salt marsh in Beaufort County is as restorative as a shot of sour-mash bourbon. The shaded streets south of Broad in Charleston can bring even Europeans to their knees. The gardens of Middleton Plantation in the springtime make you ache with pleasure. Pawleys Island is the most delightful, wondrous place in South Carolina and I envy any child who gets to grow up there.

Several years ago Albert Oliphant, a 1971 graduate of the Citadel, invited me to go up to Bamberg where his family owned a plantation with hundreds of acres bordering the Edisto River. Each year he put on a weekend outing for twenty cadets and his son at the plantation. The cadets hunted deer all day, and we sat around an outside fire at night. My curiosity concerned Albert's great-grandfather, the very famous South Carolina novelist William Gilmore Simms, who must have been the most prolific writer in the history of our state. I had read his novel about the Yemassee Indians for a history class I took at the Citadel. He also chronicled the role of South Carolina during the American Revolution and his career was long, but disappointing to him. When Albert asked me to walk with him to a small, unprepossessing building fifty yards from the big house, we could hear the cadets firing at deer from the deer stands located at intervals around the plantation. Albert held the door for me and I walked into a single room, modestly furnished with a desk and chair.

"Pat, this is the writing room where my ancestor William Gilmore Simms did most of his work," Albert said, then he added, "The last writer to be in this room that we know of occurred in 1839 when Edgar Allan Poe visited my great-grandfather when he stayed at this plantation."

There it is again—what you get over and over if you surrender yourself to South Carolina—that great surprising thing. This grand book is simply one more example of it. *State of the Heart* reminds us of what is best about South Carolina and her many gifted writers, the monumental power of this place to shape our memories into stories and then our stories into art.

Pat Conroy

Acknowledgments

Rare are those who will give away something they love, especially if they've loved it a long time. But that's what we have here, a testament to human generosity if ever there was one. Good writers are busy writers, and the superb writers represented here made time to jump into this dream. Reading these essays was like opening presents, each handmade and one-of-a-kind. My deepest gratitude to each of them, and to Pat Conroy. His bear hug of a foreword warms me each time I read it.

Likewise to the many photographers and artists who contributed their talents, and to those who helped me secure artwork and information from across the state. Reference librarians, archivists, and historians are a writer and editor's best friends. Without them, we're nothing. For more than twenty years I've called upon Beth Bilderback at the University of South Caroliniana Library and Ann Sessions at the Lexington County Public Library, and I'm so pleased to thank them here. I send another big *merci* to Lauren Virgo at the North Augusta Cultural Heritage Center, Mary Smith at the Aiken County Museum, Timothy Simmons at the Thomas Cooper Library at the University of South Carolina, Margaret Dunlap at the Richland County Public Library, Seth Withers at the Pickens County Library System, G. Anne Sheriff, curator of the Central History Museum, Allison Read at the Greenwood County Library, and Fritz Hamer, Lorrey McClure, and Elizabeth Cassidy West—also at the Caroliniana Library. I can't overlook the help of Robert Barber at Bowens Island in Charleston, Miller Murphy at the Connie Maxwell Children's Home in Greenwood, Howell Beach III with Robert Marvin/Howell Beach & Associates, Inc., in Walterboro, Loy E. Sartin, curator of the Dr. Benjamin E. Mays Historical Preservation Site in Greenwood, Mike Kohl, head of Special Collections at Clemson

University Libraries, Brian Hennessy with Clemson University's Sports Information Department, N. Adam Watson, photographic archivist with the State Archives of Florida, Bill Rogers, director of the South Carolina Press Association, Helen Benso with Brookgreen Gardens, or Linda Bowie in Sunset. Linda indulged my obsessive quest for visuals of Chapman's Bridge, a structure that lives in the hearts of the good people of the Keowee River Valley, no matter the fire that took it in 1974.

Jonathan Haupt at the University of South Carolina Press is my new hero. As they say in Hollywood, he "got behind this project" and not only made it happen, he made it so much better. Thanks to him and his staff, for their patience and expertise, and to design manager Pat Callahan. Maybe one day I'll figure out how she distilled all these words into the perfect cover design, but I doubt it.

Robin Asbury Cutler and Steve Hoffius, whose essays are included here, deserve recognition for their early encouragement. The gracious Emily Cooper and the unflappable Tracy Fredrychowski guided me through the wilderness of today's digital wonderland and kept me steady during the pre-deadline rollercoaster ride. Thanks to Bond Nickles, to whom I go with any sports-related questions, and Joey Frazier, my source for all things field-and-stream. Valuable brainstorming came via Cam Currie, Nancy Higgins, Clare Neely, and Myda Tompkins. *Reach Out, Columbia* Editor Lori Hatcher loosened other deadlines so I could meet this one. Randy Halfacre, Jennie Hatfield, and the staff at the Greater Lexington Chamber & Visitors Center have been exceptionally generous. What a great place to work.

Most of all, I must thank Maro and Hugh Rogers, who never missed an opportunity to preach to my siblings and me the necessity of knowing your history and using good grammar, and Wally Peters, who always had supper on the stove and faith this book would happen while I disappeared to put it together. They are my "acres of diamonds," and I am dazzled by the wealth.

INTRODUCTION *When the Peach Trees Bloom*

Writers are haunted people. When it comes to places, they either haunt them or are haunted by them. And there are good reasons why. Something happened there, or there's something good there, something meaningful. Sometimes there's just something about a place that puts your soul at rest. You belong there.

My soul belongs somewhere on Highway 23, between Batesburg and Edgefield. I like it especially in the early spring, when the peach trees are in bloom. I drive by, charmed and somehow soothed, by the pastel blur of orchards, so pink against the sky. They're interrupted by an occasional grand, old, unpretentious home. They seem as rooted to the earth as the farms they command. I can see myself living in one, or in any of the smaller homes along this path, from Ridge Spring and Monetta and into Ward, Johnston, and Edgefield. And I can really see myself in one of those orchards, in early spring, lying on my back, enclosed by pink.

The writers who've contributed to this book have their own special places. Some of them are South Carolina icons, famous for their history or beauty. Others are as obscure as a private back yard or hidden-in-plain-sight as a chain coffee shop. And then there are those places that no longer exist, except in the memories of those writers who can't shake them off. Haunted, they are.

But it's human to be haunted. As adults, we start understanding the pain of our parents, and their parents. They had troubles, terrific ones, and sometimes we sense this most deeply in a particular place.

So for me, the rural richness of the Ridge, that stretch of farmland where peaches grow so abundantly, calls to mind both my grandmothers. Though they came from different parts of the world, they shared a love for fruit and fruit trees. And they bore shattering tragedies they rarely talked about to their grandchildren.

Why didn't I ask them? Why is it that now when they're gone I'm curious about the things they endured? I can only research old newspapers in the Caroliniana library about the family ax murder that took the life of my grandmother's sister, causing upheaval that rattled through generations. "It was the crime of the decade," Grandmama told me once, then in her eighties. I didn't follow up. It was something we didn't talk about.

As for my other grandmother, she didn't even know her last name when, as a six-year-old, she was "marched through the desert" during the Armenian Genocide of 1915–1922. She and her older sister were the only members of her family to survive. Younger than ten, she scampered around the city of Mosul foraging for food. One of her havens was a cemetery plot where she ate grass. Medzemama's luck turned dramatically when she married the wealthy benefactor of the tent orphanage where she lived. She learned to read, speak several languages, play musical instruments. But the phrase "starving Armenian" isn't funny in our family. We know her stomach was swollen with hunger as a child.

People are shocking. They do mean things to each other. It happens all the time, to all of us. When it happens to me, I head for that two-lane road that carries me through those orchards and towns, where I perceive peace to be. I know there's drama in the fair counties of Saluda and Edgefield; they have indeed had their share of well-documented strife. But when the peach trees are in bloom, it's like snow falling on the poppies in *The Wizard of Oz*. Life seems to settle down and at the same time, promise something good.

Grandmama and Medzemama left their mark. My mother haunts the farmers market in Columbia, recreating, I think, the markets of her childhood in Iraq. Boxes of grapefruit are the family reward. My father, no matter how hot it is, returns to his Lexington County homeplace every summer to pick figs. Famously fast to get off the farm, he nevertheless refuses to let a single fig go to waste. I can't remember a time when we didn't have fig preserves.

Many people visualize a beach when they can't sleep. But I see myself driving to peach country, pulling off the side of the road and then running, fast, fast, fast, to the peace I imagine is there. And then I find an orchard, an old one, with gnarly trees in wild profuse bloom. I enter it, and my grandmothers are with me. We lie down, and they tell me the stories I was too new to the world to understand. The sun is shining, and a breeze is blowing. All around us is pink. We talk and we talk, and we laugh and we sing. And then we rest.

Sullivan's Island Lighthouse.
Art by Lowry Coe, courtesy of Lowcountry Sketches.

The Beckoning

Near the Doorway

There may have been
An empty road, opening
Its hands for me.

Standing in the center of a field,
I watched fog spreading over the island
As layers of clouds streamed
Overhead. Birds in the trees
Were calling out to one another.

I couldn't tell their voices apart.
I couldn't see which branches they were calling from.

Looking down, I dreamed the earth
Was one field emptied of fog,

One house near the sea.

I began to walk.
Dark fires burned along the shore road.

Four flames
Four directions
Salt tossed in the wind.

Rain fell at my feet
Snow fell, far off.
Stone, star, cold, fire.

The birds suddenly silent
In the trees. I saw my voice. ☽

Marjory Wentworth

A Most Unexpected Muse

This is a story about a natural disaster, a flooded home, and a displaced family; but it's also a story about resurrection from the ruins. It is, therefore, a quintessentially southern story. It is the story of my family's life on Sullivan's Island—the place we raised our children with a freedom that few children still experience—where they rolled out of bed every morning, put on their backpacks, walked across the street past the Poe Library, and went to school with a view of the ocean. After school, they arrived home to a door facing the sea that was always open, because we never had a key. The island was their playground, from Stella Maris Church to the bamboo forest on the hill, from Breech Inlet to Officers Row; and that's where our three little boys, hair bleached blond by the sun, played their hearts out every single day of their childhood. At Fort Moultrie, they could run through the tunnels to escape the British. On the backside of the island they built a fort in the marsh grass. In our endless back yard they had a swing set and a sandbox, trees for climbing, and a garden bursting with cucumbers, okra, tomatoes and watermelon. They spent endless days at the beach, where they swam almost year-round, built sand castles, caught crabs, went boogie boarding and surfed. Those days, rolling one on top of the other, are a continuous dream of childhood.

Like many people you meet in Charleston, we just kind of landed here. We were looking to move out of our Brooklyn apartment when my husband Peter was offered a job with a film company based in Charleston. When we first moved to Sullivan's Island that summer of 1989, it was still a funky place filled with old run-down beach houses that had been in families for generations, and it had a small-town feel that appealed to us after living in the city for a decade. In those days, there was no Isle of Palms connector, no five-thousand square foot mansions, Mr. Gruber still ran "The Wishing Well," an old convenience store, and houses cost less than $200,000. Everyone seemed to know everyone else. We bought a run-down gatehouse on Middle Street with a huge back yard where our sons could play. It was built in 1853 and had survived hurricanes, earthquakes, and the Civil War. Although the air conditioning was spotty, the windows wouldn't open, and there were leaks in the roof and only one closet, the house had a charm that suited us. The minute we walked in the front door, we were home.

Since the island is only a half-mile wide, the sense of the sea was palpable. Even though we could only see the ocean from the third floor "crow's nest," we could always smell the salt and hear the waves moving on shore. The lighthouse was only a couple of blocks away, and at night the great light would shine into our bedrooms as it made its never-ending circle. After a few nights, the light became a comforting presence.

I grew up in a small coastal town north of Boston, and I am used to being lulled to sleep by the sound of foghorns, but truth be told I had always felt an awkward sense of estrangement from my homeplace. Although both my family and my husband's family have lived in New England for centuries, I knew I belonged somewhere else. I just didn't know where that was. I could never have imagined it would be anyplace south of the Mason-Dixon Line, but so it goes.

In New England, the same metal-colored sky can last for months at a time, especially in early winter. On Sullivan's Island at sunset, the sky turned from yellow to pink a million different ways. The light falling upon the earth here must be like the light shining in heaven. The landscape was exotic, lush, and sensual. Palmetto and banana trees were scattered through the back yard that took up two lots. Trumpet vine climbed the fences. Everything was blooming in the thick humid air that summer before Hurricane Hugo. As a poet, I was dazzled. I love New York, but the entire time I lived there I craved nature. Like many poets, I look to the natural world for meaning and metaphors.

We were still unpacking boxes and getting to know our neighbors when we had to evacuate for Hurricane Hugo that September. We had so little time to board up the house and pack the car that we didn't have time to find the box with our sons' birth certificates. We knew the hurricane was coming straight for us. Nothing would ever be the same for our family or this small island we had just started to call home.

Two days after Hurricane Hugo made landfall, we drove back from Columbia on Route 26, not knowing what we would find, if anything.

Rumors were circulating that all the barrier islands were still covered in water. We were terrified. There were hardly any cars on the road. Things looked fairly normal until we got about thirty miles outside of Charleston. None of the traffic lights worked because there was no power. The entire forest on either side of the highway had been flattened by the high winds. Every single tree trunk was snapped in two. It looked like bombs had been dropped. We drove with the windows down, and the absence of sound was haunting. The hum of everyday life was missing in the air. Whenever we passed a clump of people waiting in line for water or food, the silence continued. It was as if people were too shocked to speak to one another. We just kept going.

The National Guard seemed to be everywhere in Charleston. We hitched a boat ride out to Sullivan's Island, since the Ben Sawyer Bridge was flipped open during the storm. When we got off the Boston Whaler near Station 24, we got a ride down Middle Street in one of their trucks. Since so many wires were down it was dangerous to walk anywhere. There were lots of people in the back of the truck. One woman was crying uncontrollably, another woman vomited over the side. The truck stopped about a quarter of a mile from our house, because another house was in the middle of the road and there was no way to drive around it. We couldn't see beyond the wreckage. A man took my hand when we climbed out of the back and said "May God be with you." Peter and I ran down the street, hurtling over tree trunks and garbage cans. Our eight-month-old son Oliver was in a backpack and he thought this part was funny. And suddenly there was our house. Hallelujah. The live oak in the front yard hadn't crushed our roof. The yard was filled with smashed muddy furniture, someone's dishwasher, surfboards, and lawn chairs—just endless wet stuff tangled in the downed tree limbs. One block over, a tornado took out every single home in its path. We felt lucky.

Inside was another story. Every single thing was covered in wet mud and sand. Every piece of furniture, every dish, every spoon. The tidal surge had left two and half feet of mud on the first floor. The smell of mold and mildew was overwhelming. It would last for months. My husband's brothers flew down from Maine with their chainsaws. They did their best to clean up, but by the end of October electricity was sporadic at best.

We tried moving back home. Neighbors had left baby food and a box of diapers at our front door. We ate meals served by the Red Cross at the Baptist church down the road. Donations came in from all over the country. Our four-year-old son Hunter was overjoyed to find boxes of his favorite

Kraft macaroni and cheese. The Red Cross lady gave Hunter six boxes. Black marker messages were written in a child's scrawl across the blue and yellow cardboard. "From the children of Toledo, Ohio," one read. Another had a personal note: "I hope you like macaroni and cheese as much as I do." It was signed like a letter—"your friend, Amy." Another box that I saved said "we are praying for you in Alabama." Was this my life? Helicopters flew overhead. All day long the sound of chainsaws filled the air. It was beyond chaotic.

It just wasn't safe to stay in our house on Middle Street. The ceilings were filled with water and the basic structure of the house was not sound. We settled into a condominium on the Isle of Palms that my friend Louisa found for us. There were sheets and towels and pots and pans, and the electricity and running water worked all the time. Finally, we could settle down and begin to rebuild our lives. That winter we hired a contractor to replace floors and walls and the thousands of other things that needed to be done to make the home habitable. By spring, most of the debris was picked up along the road side, both lanes of the Ben Sawyer Bridge were finally working, and everywhere you looked something was blooming. I had never seen such abundance—honeysuckle, wild roses, and Carolina jessamine crawling wild along every fence filling the air with scent.

After eight months, thanks to our neighbors, we were able to move back to Sullivan's Island to the little blue gingerbread house almost next door to our house, which was months away from completion. But, finally, we were back home on the island where our newfound friends lived.

That summer after Hurricane Hugo, day-to-day life finally took on a kind of normalcy. I was pregnant with our third son Taylor, and I began to write poems again. I felt an intense connection with the landscape that I would not have had if we hadn't seen it virtually destroyed only months earlier. As construction began on our house, my belly grew, and the land itself seemed to be healing. The poems I wrote had an underlying emotional intensity. I never considered myself a landscape poet, but I clung to the imagery surrounding me on the island and I wrote my way out of the pain that characterized that year. Funny how life works, but the poems eventually formed a book called *Noticing Eden* and I began my life as a published poet.

Our attachment to Sullivan's Island, which is fierce and hard earned, is hard to explain and still difficult to talk about because we no longer call this fragile barrier island our home. The roof leak was never really fixed, the walls were never completely dried out, and the endless problems with mold and termites just wore us down. When Hunter graduated from high school, we waved the white flag and moved to Mt. Pleasant to a home with heating and air conditioning in every room. But for us and many others who lived through Hurricane Hugo, it will always be home. Sullivan's Island is a most unexpected muse, and despite everything I am eternally grateful. ☽

"Finest of Foods"
Edwin Turner's
Chicken Basket
Florence,
South Carolina

Edwin Turner's
CHICKEN BASKET

Courtesy of South Caroliniana Library,
University of South Carolina, Columbia.

Counters, Barstools and Booths

EDWIN TURNER'S CHICKEN BASKET
Serving the Finest of Foods in an attractive atmosphere. Enjoy your meals
in our Knotty Pine Dining Room. Or use our excellent curb service and
eat in your own car . . . 1 miles south of Florence, S.C., on U.S. 301
and 52.

For the Love of Dogs

Several years ago, I was having one of those days, the kind that makes a person want to escape—the kind that evokes memories of Grandma's kitchen and kicks off a desperate search for a new source of comfort.

With that in mind, I decided to go to my favorite bar. Typically, I didn't go alone, but at two o'clock in the afternoon, I had no other choice. Most of my friends were at work. I picked a stool, threw my purse on the counter and told the lady behind it to "keep 'em coming." By five o'clock, I was at home and feeling much more hopeful.

A couple of weeks later, a friend—curious about my allegedly mood-altering hangout—decided to join me there. We started by ordering two each, but I had no intention of stopping there. About forty-five minutes later, I noticed the smiling face of a young man peering in my direction from the kitchen area beyond the bar. There weren't many customers that summer afternoon, so the establishment lacked its normal diner-type buzz.

As he began to point at me, I could swear I heard him say something like, "That's her. That little girl right there. She's the one who had six last time she was here."

"How dare he?" I balked. I had five—and asked for two more to go.

My friend giggled, made a few tasteless remarks about "my problem," and exhibited envy that I could eat so many hot dogs so fast with little regard for calories—or dignity.

I offered a matter-of-fact explanation: "Some people drink, others do drugs, I have dogs—Just Dogs."

Since then, Just Dogs in Greenville's Cherrydale Plaza has been my unsurpassed go-to spot. It doesn't serve alcohol, but those who've tried the food at this amazing eatery would gladly give up fine wine for a smoked sausage

Gary Thomas and Amanda Capps buddy it up at Just Dogs.
Photograph by Steven Faucette.

dog on a six-inch sub roll with roasted peppers, mushrooms, onions, and savory spices smothered in Swiss and cheddar cheese.

Gary Thomas opened Just Dogs in 2001. Creativity was at the heart of his success and satisfaction when he worked with his father in the home-building industry. Now folks marvel at his custom-crafted spices, and others return again and again for the foundation of his talents: the basic hot dog.

True connoisseurs know that subtle differences in this deceptively simple American staple determine whether the dining experience warms the heart or burns it. The classic dog, Gary believes, is defined by both its ingredients and its preparation. "It takes more than one thing to make a good hot dog," he says. "You start with a hot dog made from quality beef and pork and you serve it on a fresh steamed bun with good chili. All of it has to be there."

Gary credits his parents with good chili recipes, but insists his is the one that has been perfected for the restaurant. It's an old-fashioned beanless chili—not too sweet, not too spicy. Remarkably nongreasy, it's the perfect complement to the food. Customers undergoing cancer treatments and those with other health conditions that might preclude eating hot dogs have said the ones at Just Dogs don't upset their stomachs.

"That's not a scientific claim," he cautions. "I have been told that though, and all I can say is that every day, I ask the Lord to bless the food here. I won't open the doors until I do."

More than ever, Gary and his family have relied on their faith to keep the business going. His son, J.T., the good-natured employee who had once given me that much-needed laugh at myself, was killed in a car accident in 2008. His death at twenty-four thwarted plans to open a second restaurant in Easley, and his absence has a noticeably profound effect on his father. Like the twinge of gray in his beard, the sadness in his eyes marks wisdom and strength.

Gary and his employees treat everyone like family, and that's no slogan. It's more than good manners and attentive service. If they call you "honey" and "sweetie," they mean it. The soda fountain décor, with an autograph wall for local and national sports figures and lots of NASCAR memorabilia, adds to the friendly atmosphere. And the fried bologna, homemade apple pies, and chowchow are reminiscent of a southern kitchen from a bygone era.

I take comfort at Just Dogs, probably because it conjures my first daycare center. Capps Automotive Machine, my dad's workplace in Laurens, was where a Barbie could turn a wrench and hot dogs—never without steamed buns and chili—were lunch at least twice a week. When we didn't have dogs, we went to a mom-and-pop gas station with a meat and three attached. In my experience since then, "the kind of food Grandma used to make" rarely can be found on a menu, and when it is, the fare doesn't measure up to home cooking.

Just Dogs is an exception. If they start serving potato biscuits and blackberry pie, I'll have to move in! ☽

"Please Tip the Oysterman"

Were I to choose a place in South Carolina I love more than the city of Charleston, with its ability to rest and soothe the eye at the same time it offers previously unnoticed curves and lines, steeples and rooftops, I would have to choose the blousy and beautiful Bowens Island. I am not one to choose favorite places. I usually like where I am, hate to move, and then when in the new place settle in as comfortably as a cat on the best sofa.

But I heard more about Bowens Island before I came to Charleston than I had heard about the state itself. My friend Marion Sullivan, when I was writing *New Southern Cooking,* sharply rebuked something I wrote about oysters. "In South Carolina every cove is known for a different oyster," she informed me. "Don't go making sweeping generalizations about something as important as oysters."

I knew the Southern Apalachicola oysters intimately, having roasted them outside, eaten them cold from icy coolers. I knew some Savannah oysters, eating them one cold night in particular at a charity party with a host of celebrities. Our hands were cold as we grasped the hot oysters and pried them open, pouring their juices down our throats to warm us before sliding the oysters down to warm our bellies.

At the time, I couldn't find many restaurants that sold South Carolina oysters. It was always an anathema to me how it was impossible to get local seafood in the coastal restaurants of Georgia, Florida and South Carolina unless it were fried. One could meet the boats and buy off the dock, but not dine on local seafood in a restaurant. Bowens Island was the anomaly, and that made it all the more memorable.

When I first ate there, as the guest of friends who knew my love of fresh seafood and my disinclination for pretentious dining, we got lost.

The late John Sanka taking a break.
Photo by Cramer Gallimore.

Most people get lost going to Bowens Island, I suspect. I know it now by a deserted boat on the right side of Folly Road that has constantly changing graffiti on its side. If the boat disintegrates I shall be lost again. Just a few hundred yards past the boat is a small, seemingly begrudging sign announcing the restaurant and to turn right. If unnoticed, you can wind up lost and confused. The rough, paved road continues as a causeway through the marsh and becomes a bumpy dirt road as it enters the woods on Bowens Island proper. Suddenly, now, there are beautiful homes, homes with views that rival those anywhere. Following the road to its end, looming out of nowhere, is the restaurant. Drive any farther and you wind up in the salt marshes leading to the sea or run into waist-high mounds of oyster shells, evidence of past diners.

Before the days when I didn't care who owned a restaurant, I just wanted to eat what I wanted to eat, and that was fresh oysters, cooked just like I knew from beach and other outside oyster roasts, but *inside*. Walking into Bowens Island restaurant in those days—the 1970s, I suppose—was like traveling back to my youth. The order was taken by an old man (John Sanka was his name) sitting behind a long Coca-Cola drink box, money paid on the spot. There was another cooler with ice and cold drinks and spigots adorning rough containers containing sweet tea and water. If ordering something fried—shrimp or fish, for instance, or hush puppies—it was possible to glimpse the order sliding into the fat in the iron skillet, watch the fat bubble up and hear the sizzle. Noses wrinkled and mouths tingled, anticipating the brown crusty exterior of the hush puppies and their tender moist interiors. The aroma of the fresh shrimp—cooked every whichaway—would sway many an oyster lover into ordering both.

A four-foot-tall wooden-framed radio, much like the one I sat in front of as a child in the 1940s listening to *The Shadow,* was against one wall. The ornate pieces of wood that kept the cloth in place over the speakers were broken, and the radio seemed unembarrassed to be so displayed, receiving instead the homage due its age. It was surrounded by other dismembered televisions and radios, framed prints and paintings holding dust to their surfaces as if it were an unmovable patina. A 1940s jukebox still worked, sort of, and gave you five plays of 78 rpm records for a quarter. The room had rows of wooden tables with holes cut out of their middles so oyster and shrimp shells, napkins and other debris could be shoveled into the trash-cans underneath. Even then the walls and furniture were lined with graffiti, phone numbers of ladies and strumpets, four-letter words and praise for the oysters. The women's room, even at that time, seemed prewar, with little capacity for flushing.

In the Oyster Room there was an open fireplace, the fire licking at oysters covered with a wet burlap cloth to steam them open. Sitting down at one of those same tables, hush puppies ready in a flash, I could watch the oysters brought in by the oysterman who cooked them.

Dumped from a broad shovel on newspaper before I had a chance to read it and clustered together in piles, dinner was on the table. Hot sauce, saltines, a cold drink, a few towels, a two-ounce soufflé cup, and an oyster knife accompanied the oysters. Clusters challenge the diner, and I was no exception. But once pried open, they rival any other local oyster. No sense in talking, the eating is so good.

That was not the entire restaurant, of course. Outside was more—an enclosed dock room over the water, a screened porch and fireplace in the far background. Docks on either side beckoned a walk out over the marsh. A wooden walkway goes into the dock room, chairs and tables scattered, with a breathtaking view. A hard decision is whether to eat there, watching the boats coming into the dock and feeling the breeze, or to go back and watch the oysters being cooked.

Henry Gaillard shoveling succulents in the Oyster Room in 2006, before the fire. Photograph by Cramer Gallimore.

In his book *Southern Food* John Edgerton describes the previous owners, the Bowens, so beautifully I wish I knew them when they lived on this fourteen-acre island. Southern Foodways Alliance has done oral histories with the local oystermen who know exactly where to find the secret oyster beds and bring the oysters in every morning. In 2006, the James Beard Foundation gave the restaurant a medal. The present owner, the Bowens' grandson, Robert Barber, sat on the stage in New York in his oyster boots and praised his oystermen, accepting the award on their behalf. For it is they who have kept the tradition of local oysters alive for the sixty-plus years the restaurant has been open. Countless articles, from the *New York Times* and other national and local media, have praised it.

One night in October 2006, shortly after Bowens Island received the James Beard award, a fire burnt a good part of the restaurant down. The grief in Charleston—and the wider southern food community—was palatable. To the delight of many, the restaurant was closed only three months and a week. A new kitchen was built in an adjacent building. On the dock and deck that survived the fire, the staff served their regular customers, as well as hosted the SFA and other groups, parties, and special friends while the construction went on around what was left.

In August 2010, all was rebuilt. Now with handicapped access, Bowens Island Restaurant is an even better place for all who love local oysters and some of the best fried seafood anywhere. Graffiti is already around. The sign "Please Tip the Oysterman"—he *is* the one who stokes the fire and shovels the oysters—is roughly scrawled on one wall. Panoramic views of water, marshes, islands, dolphins, birds, and sky are better than ever. The original building, grandfathered in before modern building codes and perhaps even state regulations, was oblivious to design, rambling as it chose. The rebuilding involved all the codes the previous restaurant was able to ignore. The result of the new construction is a simple elevated building, built to LEED green building standards. And the pleasure is still there, that of jabbing the oyster knife into the shells of the clusters of oysters, pulling out the still-dripping oysters, sipping the juices and letting the oyster slide down the throat. May it long last, past my time and others, and bring the island and its prized ambiance to the rest of the oyster lovers of South Carolina. ☽

Sipping from the Secret Cup

For a year, almost every morning I sat by the window at Panera for an hour, ate a bagel and sipped half-and-half iced tea, watched the sun rise over the cemetery, and wrote (on brown napkins) small poems about big abstractions having to do with God, love, and death. It was a time of soul searching and soul hiding, of observing and imagining, of accomplishing and failing.

What I'm saying is that one of my favorite places in South Carolina is the Hillcrest Panera in Spartanburg. It's embarrassing. Surely I have a favorite shady rock on the bank of the Lawson's Fork, or a serene waterfall on the Green River, or a grassy knoll with a majestic view of Mt. Mitchell . . . or even a golf course, or a beach. . . . But Panera is where I went every day and where I still go often, and I cherish my time there. It's a clean, well-lighted place, it smells like fresh-brewed coffee and fresh-baked bread, the women who get me my bagel—Sylvia, Margaret, Sonya, Christine—are always pleasant (they know my name, but I like it even better when they call me Hon), and I could eat a fresh, warm bagel every morning of my life and not get tired of them. But it's the combination of these pleasant amenities and the magic of early morning that makes transcendence possible at Panera.

I tend to wake up early, and because my head is usually full of practical and impractical static as soon as my dreams and their echoes fade away, I can't go back to sleep, so I go to Panera when it opens at 6:30 A.M. For part of the year, it's dark then, for part it's light, but throughout the year, if I sit from 6:30 to 7:30, I behold one of the 365 scenes of the transition from night to day. To state what is obvious to me: God doesn't create the world anew each day, but the world changes each day as the sun, moon, earth, and stars move in relation to each other, affecting light, temperature, and the disposition of all living things.

I look forward to this time, and my disposition is generally good, open, expectant. In cold weather I'm disposed to sit in one of the leather arm chairs by the warm and mesmerizing fire (although now they've moved those chairs over to the window), but I also have a vista to the north, across the parking lot, up to East Main and beyond. Islands of crape myrtles (deep pink all summer) and liriope dot the lot; and on the clearest days, the faint impressions of the old, worn, mountains of the Blue Ridge rise above the trees.

In mild weather I sometimes sit outside, but I usually sit in a booth by a side window looking east over the parking lot to the gap between the movie theater and a hedge through which I can see a slice of Greenlawn Memorial Gardens, where all four of my Greek-immigrant grandparents and many other relatives are buried. I can't see their particular graves from where I sit, but I see them every day as I drive past or take a walk in that direction, so I'm well connected to my past if I want to wander or wonder there.

With this quiet and comfortable world available to my senses, my thoughts drift aimlessly, usually along the lines of my sight, until they find a tether or focus, and I write haiku. Haiku is a Japanese form of poetry consisting of three lines of five, seven, and five syllables (although the Japanese don't seem to be strict about the syllable count) that presents an image of nature and often includes a spiritual element. They don't usually rhyme, but mine usually do because the music appeals to me. Although I wasn't fully conscious of it as I was writing them, mine are Sufi-like. In them I often address a "you," an omni-being, God, loved one . . . and I tentatively call the poems "You Haiku." When I mentioned that to Coleman Barks, the masterful translator of the Persian poet Rumi, he said, "That's very Sufi." In the introduction to his collection "Open Secrets," Coleman wrote about the mystery of the *you* Rumi addresses—is it a person, a divinity, "the inner, angelic counterpart," or all the above?—and when Coleman spoke at Wofford College, he described the Sufi "you" further, after which I wrote this haiku based on his description:

You, Persian pronoun—
kindness, laughter, sadness, fire—
you, my secret cup.

I use that "you" liberally and fluidly. Most often it's meant to represent an elusive and ethereal being whom I long for, especially on those dark mornings that are more night than day:

The full moon rises,
a white balloon, surrenders—
morning without you.

Sometimes he-she-it is there in my sense of the day, but in the margins:

Even gray and grim
the scrim of winter heaven
has you embroidered.

Sometimes the you is the show, and the religious tone is clear:

Your disciple soil
brings offerings, little greens—
your gospel is spring.

But sometimes I leave you out of it and devote all my syllables to natural things:

Fairy rings, beetle
wings, morning dew, bursting buds,
lightning bugs—spring's bling.

Sometimes I'm guardedly optimistic in the face of day.

Nature's fallacy—
morning rain, agnostic sky,
but I know you're there.

But I express a lot more doubt than faith, and the you is absent more often than present. I think it's partly because my default mood is melancholy, and my morning ritual at Panera was a lonely enterprise, and I enjoyed simmering in sadness and sipping from the secret cup.

After all, I was usually looking at graves, being reminded of my mortality and the terrifying thought that at the end of this mortal coil there is . . . nothing. But graves are markers—something, someone is here in this place, whether he or she is bones, or dust, or just memory—and that something/ someone is an antidote for the terror of nothingness. When I walk in or gaze at the cemetery, I always think about my grandparents. I do that in part because I've been writing a book about the Greeks of the Upstate, and my grandparents figure prominently; but I also do it because, well, that's what cemeteries are for: they're a place to bury your loved ones, to honor and immortalize them by carving their names in stone, and to mark the

Deno Trakas conjuring haiku.
Photograph by Mark Olencki.

spot so you can visit. Something of them "remains" there, but we also hope that their spirits have moved on to Heaven. Isn't that what we need most from religion? Belief in permanence, belief in an afterlife?

Belief is like love without the hormones. It comes to me not from church or religious doctrine but from the evidence of God in nature that we usually take for granted; it comes not from the stone cross near my grandparents' graves inscribed in Greek with words that mean "I expect/believe in the resurrection" but from the oak tree nearby, the centipede grass, the temperate air that sustains us with every breath . . . and the miracle of making bread and butter from grain and milk. For me, there is no better affirmation of life and evidence of the existence of God than bread and butter. And no better place to put a Panera than next to a cemetery.

I'm trying to sound like I know what I'm talking about, but I don't. I have friends who walk firmly on the earth and seem certain about all kinds of things, even God and love, but I constantly wobble. I'm rich in love and yet don't have enough. I'm rich in doubt yet pray when I visit the graves of my relatives. Life is precious because of death, and life is painful, sometimes almost intolerable, because of death. There are two sides (or more) to everything.

I like haiku because it wears ambiguity well. And I like Panera because it bakes bread all day, and early in the morning it's a perfect place to recollect emotions in tranquility, which, according to Wordsworth, is what poetry is all about.

I didn't write dates on the haiku, and I have no clear idea of when I began writing them or when I stopped. I had almost a hundred, but I threw away a lot of them. I still eat at Panera frequently, and I still write haiku occasionally, but that intense, soul-searching phase is over.

Not that I've found my soul—it's as elusive as ever. In fact, I'm at Panera now and don't see any sign of it on this gray midsummer morning, so I'm working on this essay instead of writing haiku. I think about what I've said, and I find myself falling into my old habit of counting syllables on my fingers.

"Belief is like love." Five syllables—perfect for a first line. I feel haiku coming and look out the window for a fitting image and listen in my head for a natural rhyme. I open a brown napkin and write, trying to mean many things without meaning nothing, feeling satisfaction and disappointment, coming up with three lines that are cryptic and imperfect:

Belief is like love—
the sun rising behind clouds,
blinding when it breaks. ☽

Anna Hyatt Huntington Modeling "The Torchbearers," by Herbert Bohnert
(1890–1967). Oil on canvas, 1958. Collection of Brookgreen Gardens,
gift of Anna Hyatt Huntington.

Chasing Tranquility

"I must tell you about our one day at Brookgreen while it is fresh in my mind, else all that we have seen since will dim it . . . The old garden looked even more attractive and a low bush of japonica was in bloom and very lovely . . . I felt a strong impulse to sit on the porch and not go back to the boat."

From a letter sculptor Anna Hyatt Huntington (1876–1973) wrote her sister in 1930, after her husband Archer bought the property that would become Brookgreen Gardens

Weekend with Sadie

My daughter was four years old the first time we camped at Calhoun Falls State Park in western Abbeville County. We threw our tent into the back of the truck, left Mom at home with a new baby, and headed out for a couple of days of daddy-daughter time. I think back on our first camping weekend and smile. Little did I know that not only would I include my son in this experience when he got older, but we (including Mom) would make camping at Calhoun Falls a family tradition.

Sadie was just learning to read that chilly weekend in March 2005. Much of our time was spent sitting around the campfire reading books, working on our rock-skipping skills on a lake still too cold for swimming, and wandering the nature trails before evening's chill sent us back to camp and a warm fire.

"Daddy, what does that sign say?" Sadie asked as we walked along the road near our campsite.

Always on the lookout for a teaching moment, I answered with a question of my own. "What do you think it says? Sound out the letters."

With only a brief struggle, Sadie quickly got the first word. "'Wildlife.' But I don't know the second word," she said.

"What about the last word?"

She played around with the possible vowel sounds before deciding that the word was "area."

"Good job," I said. "Now, let's try to sound out the middle word together."

Sadie muttered various pronunciations to herself, her eyes wide with the array of possibilities. She moved closer to the sign, and before I could offer any further advice, she turned back to me with a wide grin.

Shane Bradley and his children at Calhoun Falls State Park.
Photograph by Sharon Bradley.

"Wait!" she yelled. "I've got it. It says 'Wildlife Enchantment Area!'"

I laughed, then hugged the child who was already hooked on fairy tales and princesses. Yes, I told her that the sign actually marked a field beginning to show spots of green that had been designated a Wildlife *Enhancement* Area, and that we might see a deer or a rabbit or a raccoon bounding about the open field. Or, we could watch birds that came there to peck the spring ground for insects. But since that day, after countless campouts in almost every month of the year, the Wildlife "Enchantment" Area has become a cherished part of our family outdoor experience. Not a trip to the park goes by that we don't reminisce about Sadie's pronunciation error, a mistake that has helped define our family time ever since.

For many people, Calhoun Falls State Park really is a wildlife enchantment area. There's something refreshing, invigorating about spending time away from the distractions of everyday life. The scent of pine and aroma of campfire smoke greet you immediately. Whitetail deer roam with the ease that comes from years of unmolested freedom. I think every campsite must have a resident squirrel that slinks up to picnic tables for handouts before retreating back to the safety of a tree to wait for another tasty morsel.

Because the U.S. Army Corps of Engineers maintains control of the lake and most of the surrounding shoreline, development remains virtually nonexistent on Lake Richard B. Russell. A boat ride along the old Rocky River, past the Seaboard train trestle into the former Savannah River and under the Highway 72 bridge down to Richard B. Russell Dam, is like slipping back in time. An osprey warns that you might be a little too close to her nest, fish leap about in the morning stillness of secluded coves, and deer look on with alert stares from the orange clay bank. That sound you hear is the water lightly lapping against the bridge pylons.

We love the cool mornings of early spring or fall, when we take leisurely walks on the two miles of nature trails. Robust hikers can trek around the cove-laced shoreline, which reveals hidden sandy banks, a diversity of water birds, raccoons scavenging for breakfast, and unfettered access to the more uncharted parts of the 26,650-acre Lake Russell that most visitors will never see.

At the end of the day, the sun seems to melt into Georgia behind a shimmering tree-lined horizon, signaling the moon and stars that their time to take the grand stage has come. The glow of camping lights brightens evening walks, and a cool breeze blowing off the lake pushes back the day's heat. The smells of chicken, burgers, and steaks browning on the grill, and fresh fish frying in the pan stir the appetite after a day of outdoor enjoyment. It doesn't get much better than this.

We've learned to make our reservations far in advance, because campsites and shelters go fast. We've also learned the folks at the park store are gracious, and will lend you racquets and balls for tennis and basketball. Camping neighbors are friendly, and Sue in the office is always glad to help us or anyone get settled.

Sadie is ten years old now, and every excursion to the 315-acre park includes laughter-filled recollections of the Wildlife Enchantment Area. Her brother, a rough-and-tumble six-year-old, doesn't understand all the fuss over an enchanted field, but you know how boys are. He would much rather be building sandcastles on the huge beach at the swimming area or sliding face-down the sliding board at one of the playgrounds.

The American Romantic writer Washington Irving wrote about his need to find an escape from the "sordid, dusty, soul-killing way of life" created by our desire to have more and be more. A trip to Calhoun Falls State Park is one idea for soul nourishment. For me, this is where I can let my cares fade into the morning mist rolling across the lake, and lose my troubles deep along a forest trail. With a little practice, who knows? I might be able to recover some of that childlike magic Sadie reminded us of so well. ☽

Big Woods

I first visited Congaree National Park in 1967, nine years before it became open to the public as part of the National Park System. Back then the park was a private hunt club, owned by a family-held timber company from Chicago. I was a sophomore in college, home for Easter weekend, and a guest of hunt club member and well-known conservationist Harry Hampton. I was here because as a youngster I had developed a strong love of nature and the outdoors, whetted by growing up on the edge of Columbia in a still-young subdivision called Forest Acres that was full of vacant woodlots and empty fields. A love of reading steered me to books on wildlife and wild America. I learned that so much of our natural heritage had been squandered and exhausted. This was in the late 1950s and early '60s, well before Earth Day and the modern environmental movement.

I was particularly fascinated by the virgin forests that once covered the south—the great swamp hardwood forests with canopies so tall and dense that the noonday sun was blotted out, and the endless expanses of longleaf pine that stretched from southern Virginia to eastern Texas. I was saddened and felt cheated to read about extinct wildlife that once thrived in these forests—the panthers, wolves, ivory-billed woodpeckers, Carolina parakeets, passenger pigeons, all lost; gone, along with the primeval forests that sustained them.

Imagine my surprise then, when I saw a photograph in *South Carolina Wildlife* magazine of Harry Hampton standing by the biggest bald cypress tree I had ever seen. And I was even more surprised when, after writing Mr. Hampton, he replied that this was not just a single tree or grove of trees, but one of many big trees found within a fifteen-thousand-acre tract of pristine

John Cely measuring a 29-foot buttress of a bald cypress in Congaree National Park. It's the largest known buttress in the park. Photograph by Joe Kegley.

bottomland hardwood forest along the Congaree River just a few miles south of Columbia.

This set the stage for my first trip to the Congaree. It was a beautiful April morning and Mr. Hampton showed me a magnificent hardwood forest that I thought existed only in history books. I marveled at sweet gums that were 5 feet in diameter, cherrybark oaks with buttresses that measured more than twenty feet around, and loblolly pines fifteen stories high. Many of the trees were so tall we needed binoculars to identify the leaves that were so far away up in the canopy.

Scientists were to learn later that Congaree National Park supports one of the tallest hardwood forests in the temperate world. Here in an undisturbed forest where Nature called the shots and trees were allowed to live a natural life span, some trees exceeded 150 feet in height. Even the lowly persimmon, normally a weedy tree of old fields and road edges, achieved gigantic proportions at Congaree, with heights of more than 120 feet. Years later, forest scientists measured a national champion loblolly pine at Congaree and found it to be almost 170 feet tall, or seventeen stories high, the tallest known tree in South Carolina.

Mr. Hampton's sixty-nine-year-old legs walked my nineteen-year-old legs off that spring morning. He was a tall, lean man who moved effortlessly through the forest, but even his six-foot, three-inch frame was dwarfed by the big trees of the Congaree. I remember on the drive back to Columbia how puny the woodlands passing by our vehicle seemed. I had seen the real thing, a living relic truly deserving the name "forest," a forest of which William Faulkner would have been proud and one worthy of ivory-billed woodpeckers and Carolina parakeets.

Since 1967, I have spent countless hours exploring and discovering the Congaree forest. In 1974 I became a foot soldier in the citizens' campaign to save the swamp from logging and have it become part of the National Park System, a campaign Harry Hampton had waged alone so tirelessly for so many years. It was truly a grassroots effort, led by a schoolteacher named Jim Elder, an engineer named Richard Watkins, a housewife named Ann Timberlake, a country lawyer named Ted Snyder, an environmentalist named Brion Blackwelder, a college professor named Robert Janiskee, an activist named Ann Jennings, and so many others that helped make a difference.

All would agree, however, that the real heroes of the campaign to save the Congaree were the hundreds of nameless individuals, young and old, who wrote letters, made phone calls, talked it up to their friends and acquaintances, and supported its protection in so many other ways. Without them there would be no Congaree National Park.

To document the national significance of the Congaree, Jim Elder and I spent many days and weeks searching the trackless forest for champion trees, the biggest of their kind. Almost as soon as we measured and submitted our tree data, we found a bigger one the next week or the next month. Some of our height measurements were off the charts and we suspected our methods were in error. Later, when foresters measured these trees with more precise instruments, we found that our errors were mostly in undermeasuring the heights.

Many of the champions we found in the 1970s have since died—from windstorms and hurricanes, lightning strikes, insects, disease, and other natural causes. But in a forest as big and diverse as the Congaree, there are many specimens almost as large as the record trees, and ready to take their place when the champions eventually die (these near champions are called Congaree's "J-V team"). Currently the park has six national champion trees and twenty-five state champions. Few areas of this size in North America can boast numbers like this.

The Congaree National Park, however, is more than just a forest of big trees. It's an extraordinarily complex and diverse ecosystem that defies traditional scientific inquiry of the "pigeon-hole" method. It is an interconnected web of soils, trees, shrubs, vines (with more species than any other park), Spanish moss, dead and down wood, animals ranging from one-celled organisms to white-tailed deer, all held together by abundant moisture and resulting in a rich stew of life referred to as "biodiversity." In some respects the Congaree is the closest thing we have to a tropical rainforest and reminds me of those I've seen in Peru, Ecuador, and Costa Rica.

The Congaree has a sense of mystery and wonder rarely found in other temperate forests. It's hard to put your finger on, but I think it must have something to do with its luxurious richness. There is a sense here of the unexpected. You anticipate something new, something different, to appear from behind the tree ahead or from the still, dark waters of a nearby gum pond, perhaps a long-vanished inhabitant of the swamp or even a species new to science.

It is a forest of sounds, full of birdsong, frog calls, insect trills and buzzes, the snorting whistle of white-tailed deer, the hoot of owls, the chatter of squirrels, the loud cry of a pileated woodpecker or red-shouldered hawk. But there is always a sound of unknown origin, a mystery sound that could be anything.

The natural sounds only highlight how quiet the park really is, which except for an occasional passing airplane, is completely devoid of the harsh noise of an increasingly loud civilization. It is a forest of solitude, a true wilderness on the back steps of Columbia, where off the trail you could go for days, if not weeks or months, and never see a soul.

This forest is a living link with our country's past. It is the forest primeval of America's early naturalists, explorers, poets, and writers. Some of the trees still standing witnessed dark clouds of migrating passenger pigeons, had flocks of Carolina parakeets roosting in their hollow trunks, and ivory-billed woodpeckers scaling their bark. Panthers and wolves prowled the ground at their bases and their roots felt the tread of moccasined Indian feet. Their leaves could have picked up the dust of Hernando De Soto's six hundred Spanish conquistadors that marched nearby nearly five hundred years ago searching for the legendary Indian village of Cofitachequi. The well-known loblolly pine by the boardwalk at Weston's Lake is referred to as the "Richland County Pine" because this one tree, perhaps the oldest loblolly pine in the world, spans the entire history of the county from its official beginnings in 1785.

Although small by National Park standards, about twenty-six thousand acres, the Congaree is really several parks in one. The park of January, when the low-angled sun of a crisp winter day streams in unimpeded to cast shadows on the forest floor, is starkly different from the densely canopied forest of July, when you are surrounded by a green wall of foliage and it's still dark at noon. The park of autumn, filled with the yellows, oranges, and reds of changing leaves, creates beauty and color found at no other time of year. The bright greens of fresh leaf growth in spring are soothing with the promise of new life. Bald cypress foliage is especially attractive in spring with its graceful, lime-colored needles that dance on the breeze like feathers.

I treasure every opportunity to visit Congaree National Park. Less than thirty minutes from my house, it never ceases to fascinate. For me it is a powerful stimulant, an enchanting green world that bombards the senses and sends the mind into overdrive with thousands of natural stimuli, large and small. No matter how often or when I go, the lasting impression is always of life, overwhelming life. ☽

The Heart of the Garden

The South Carolina Botanical Garden has a way of altering reality.
If you sit long enough in its Hosta Garden, watching huge orange fish
laze up to the surface of Heritage Pond, or if you follow its Woodland
Nature Trail far enough, enjoying the fragrance of wildflowers and the
coolness of fern-covered banks, you just might forget you're touring a
laboratory.

That's how I began a feature on the Garden well over a decade ago. Today, I
would add from my own personal experience, "you'll forget what time it is,
what year it is, what phase of life you're in. But you'll recall little sparkling
moments and feel a rush of unexpected gratitude."

I've visited the S.C. Botanical Garden at Clemson University many
times—from when it was called the "Ornamental Garden" and the "Hort
Garden" to when it became the official state garden. No matter how much
it has gained in space, programs, structures, gardens, trails, and national
acclaim—it has retained an almost mystical quality of timelessness.

For example, when I look at the Red Caboose near the Garden's entrance, twenty-five years melt away. I see myself with two young children.
I've helped them up the steep steps of the train car and onto the open space
just outside the caboose's door. My hands rest on my daughter's shoulders,
her hands on her little brother's shoulders, and we're all smiling for the
Instamatic. They are so young. I am young, again.

Or maybe, like the water running through Hunnicutt Creek or flowing
around the pond, for the moment we are ageless.

If you wander deep enough into the Garden, you'll find the "Crucible,"
an earthen sculpture beside the creek and nearly hidden in the side of a

Hunt Cabin in the Garden.
Photograph courtesy of Clemson University.

The author and her children
in the Red Caboose, 1980s.
Photograph courtesy of Liz Newall.

mossy slope. It's the first installation of the Garden's nature-based sculpture program called "Touch the Earth." You'll have to duck to enter the gnome-size doorway. But the child in you will awaken and remember how imagination once took you into worlds beyond your own.

Today, more sculptures wind through the Garden. Their names— "Chameleon Meadow," "Internal Operation," "Devotion to the Sunflower" —reveal their playfulness in a space where chronology is irrelevant. Each one, fashioned from nature and imagination, has its own story to tell.

"Clemson Clay Nest" by Nils-Udo, one of the Garden's
nature-based sculptures that has returned to the earth.
Photograph courtesy of Clemson University.

The Garden itself is a supreme example of nature-based art. More than
fifty years ago, it was another kind of monument to mankind—an abandoned campus dump. Fortunately, a Clemson horticulture professor found
it more suitable as a camellia garden. Actually, he had to move his camellia
research plot from its location near the football stadium to make way for
the stadium's expansion.

And so it began—a fraction of the space it is today—first as a camellia
garden. Then came a duck pond. From there, a public garden grew.

It gained a historical cabin and old gristmill. Then a Braille trail—where
fragrant, textured plants grow next to raised signs, all within reach of sight-
impaired visitors. Then a hortitherapy garden, the first one in the country.

And it continued to grow—powered by a mix of faithful gardeners—hor-
ticulturists, foresters, landscapers, geologists, botanists, biologists, arborists,
historians, architects, teachers, artists, musicians—and, especially, volunteers.

Now, the 295-acre site is home to a treasure of smaller gardens—"Peter
Rabbit," "Butterfly," "Cherokee Worldview," "Reflection," " Heirloom
Vegetable," "Xeriscape" and so many more. Home to meadows, trails, wildlife habitats, an arboretum. Home to historical houses, a nature-learning
center, a discovery center, a geology museum, an art gallery. And it's home

to another feature that touches my heart—the Heritage Gardens, inspired by the Class of 1939.

These days, when I go to the Garden, I tend to think about my father. He was a member of the Clemson Class of 1939. The horticulturist who started the camellia garden was his classmate. And it was his class that brought in the landmark Red Caboose, a gift from the Southern Railway depicting the young men's journey from small towns and farms to a military college and the opportunities of higher education. For many, like my father, it was their first train ride.

The 1939 alumni have nurtured the Garden throughout its growth and have established one of its most popular sites within the Garden—the Heritage Gardens—areas dedicated to displaying and honoring the history of Clemson University and the state of South Carolina. The site covers 5 acres and includes the Class of '39 Caboose Garden, the Class of '42 Golden Tiger Cadet Life Garden, Montgomery Chapel Amphitheater, a Class of '89 Picnic Area and two more legacy gardens being developed—the Presidents' Garden and the Founders' Garden. The structures, most crafted of stacked stone, blend beautifully into the nature of the landscape.

Each year, the Class of 1939 gathers in the Garden to remember classmates who passed away the previous year. A few years back, I stood near the Caboose Garden during the annual service. A '39 classmate read my father's name. He recalled meeting my father when both were college freshmen. He said that my father, who came to Clemson on a football scholarship, was the biggest man he'd ever seen at the time. Compared to today's college football players, my father would be an average-sized defensive player. But his hands would still be among the largest on the team. The chance to come to college had taken him off a Georgia farm and into a state that would become his home for the rest of his life. His scholarship paid tuition, but he worked almost year-round with those big hands—clearing tables in the cafeteria, selling peanuts at basketball games, and other odd jobs—to pay for everything else.

Academics didn't come easy to him either. He used to say he'd majored in freshman English. He actually majored in agriculture—as many did at the time. He went on to earn his degree and become a high school ag teacher. Then he earned another degree, advanced to school principal and on to district superintendent.

But he always had a garden. I remember following him down rows in the vegetable garden behind our house. He'd plow furrows in the cultivated ground. Then he would plant in a kind of rhythmic ritual. He'd drop in

C. W. "PENNY" PENNINGTON

The author's father, class of 1939. Photograph courtesy of Liz Newall.

a seed with one hand, scoop a soup can of water from a bucket with the other, pour it on the bare seed and push the soil back over the seed as gently as his huge foot could manage. Then he'd pick up the bucket, move a step forward and start again. A swooping motion, almost a dance, with the certainty that something good would take root and grow.

During that Class of 1939 service, the classmate finished speaking about my father. Someone rang a ceremonial bell, and he moved on to the next name of the newly departed. And at that moment and in this Garden, my own father was a young man again. Straight from the field and just off the train, making friends with classmates, full of strength and hope and wonder.

Maybe that's what makes this beautiful piece of upstate South Carolina so special—the sense of wonder it holds. A living preserve of past, present, future blurred together, illustrated by nature and cultivated by countless faithful gardeners.

I don't think all visitors feel the same sense of grace that I do. But I believe luminous moments await there—if you just wander deep enough. ☾

Close to the Clouds

The largest buck I ever saw hailed from Poinsett State Park in Sumter County. At the sound of my approach rounding the Coquina Trail at the back of the fishing lake, he crashed away through the swamp. Scared me much more than I scared him—about half to death.

Weirdly, that record-breaking sighting has nothing to do with my affection for Poinsett State Park. I've intruded upon deer on hiking trails all over South Carolina. We have swamps even in the upstate. There's just one Poinsett, though. It's absolutely unique.

At the breezy coquina shelter high on the park's south ridge, you're about as close to the clouds as you can walk within the coastal plain. It doesn't feel like the coastal plain at all. It feels one hundred miles north-northwest in the lower Blue Ridge. My discovery of Poinsett State Park thirty years ago was an eureka moment.

I love the mountains. From my native Lexington, mountains are a very long day trip away—more practically a weekend trip. At dawn on Saturdays, I used to drive north with a knapsack lunch, canteen and binoculars. I could be at Table Rock or on a Blue Ridge Parkway trail by nine o'clock, tromp through bear terrain until midafternoon, drive down into Greenville sweaty and weary for an early, unrushed dinner at some quiet place like Never on Sunday (that classic Greek café where they welcomed me even sweaty and weary!), and finally settle my aching frame behind the wheel to relax with folk music or Sherlock Holmes radio dramas during the long night drive home.

Those blissful escapes basically ceased after I found Poinsett, but that wasn't necessarily bad. About the only thing I missed was the Greek cuisine. At Poinsett, I found the same solitude in nature. I found the Coquina

Poinsett State Park waterworks.
Photograph by Robin Price Jumper.

Trail—comparatively short but the best approximation of invigorating mountain hiking as exists below the foothills. I found rustic little CCC cabins with their wonderful fireplace wood smoke fragrance (to me, that's a fragrance, not a smell) left courtesy the most recent renters. From my Lexington home, I could be at Poinsett in just more than an hour—a *half*-day trip. It meant I could "go to the mountains" a lot more frequently.

I did. I'd visit Poinsett on Saturdays and occasional weekdays when I was off work, but usually Sunday afternoons after church. Sometimes I'd take a notepad and work on short stories. Sometimes I'd take folkie friends with fiddle and bouzouki and concertina, and from the little shelter on the ridge we'd send Celtic reels and jigs wafting across the valley and lake below.

Most times I went alone, simply because I wanted to be alone. The only time I got distracted was when jet pilots from Shaw Air Force Base spent a couple hours on bombing practice runs over adjacent property. (*That* was loud.)

Now that we live in Spartanburg, the actual mountains are within an hour's drive; Poinsett State Park from here is almost three.

It's still my favorite place.

The coexistence of four ecosystems—sandhills, mountain terrain, hardwood forest and swampland—makes Poinsett State Park more than a little unusual, officials point out. The elevation rises from eighty feet above mean sea level (just below the lake dam) to 222 feet at the highest point. It's one of the rare places where you find a combination of flora that includes mountain laurel, Spanish moss dripping from oaks, longleaf pines and swamp cypress. The park is part of the High Hills of the Santee, a forty-mile region at the fall line, parallel to the Wateree River.

The coquina used for Poinsett's building foundations is a porous stonework believed to have originated millions of years ago. Geologists define it as fragments of ancient seashells, from the time when this was seacoast. (Coquina is Spanish for "shell.") Also of historic note are the millstones still visible from an eighteenth-century operation behind the current lake dam. The site in those days was crossed by a major road between Charleston and Camden.

Poinsett State Park is one of South Carolina's oldest, opened in 1937. (Myrtle Beach State Park opened the year before.) The park, with its five cabins, administrative buildings and shelters, is among many developed by the Civilian Conservation Corps. The CCC was one of Roosevelt's New Deal programs created to provide jobs related to recreational and conservational endeavors during the Great Depression.

Birders and other nature lovers find ample reward here. Besides hiking trails, there are courses for horseback riders and bicyclists—some fifteen trail miles, altogether. The park's trail system links to the South Carolina Palmetto Trail. The lake is a regular destination for area fishers. Families have access to multiple shaded picnic tables; groups can rent picnic shelters.

There are motorized and primitive campsites, but an extended stay for me mandates the rental of one of the cozy cabins. I relish the old-fashioned style of woodsy vacationing. Read, sleep, sit outside at night and listen to unseen wildlife, cook yourself a hardy breakfast and supper of . . . well, whatever the forest inspires you to prepare. (You wouldn't care to know what *I* cook when I'm in a place like that. At my age, cholesterol has become irrelevant.) For the benefit of campers and cabin renters, the state park service fact sheet says the nearest grocery store is eighteen miles away. That's a subjective opinion, no doubt hinged on the factician's definition of "groceries." I can find ample provisions at little stores a mite nearer.

Joel Roberts Poinsett's highest attainment as a statesman was secretary of war in President Martin Van Buren's cabinet—a historical oddity. Poinsett was no soldier. He was a doctor and a bloody botanist—an amateur botanist, but an amateur of note.

A young Charlestonian of means and refinement, a world traveler, he entered government service at age thirty. President James Madison valued his acquired knowledge of languages and foreign affairs and the friendships he'd made with royalty and various internationals in high places. Madison sent him to Argentina and Chile in 1809 to scope out the sentiments of South Americans toward the fledgling United States, as contrasted with their sentiments toward Spain, the mother country. Poinsett became probably the U.S. government's leading authority on Latin America.

Poinsett spent most of the 1820s in Mexico, initially as a government envoy, then as the first appointed U.S. minister to Mexico. In the south of the country he came upon the beautiful *Flor de Noche Buena,* or "Christmas Eve Flower," which blooms in winter. He sent specimens to the United States. Within a few years, the Poinsettia, as it was renamed, became a Christmas floral tradition.

His many roles as a statesman, culminating in the cabinet post, are less well remembered than his flower. Incidentally, he helped organize the National Institute for the Promotion of Science and the Useful Arts—one of the entities that have evolved into the Smithsonian Institution. So it is certainly appropriate that Poinsett, who died at nearby Stateburg in 1851, has this special natural attraction named for him.

It had been six and a half years since I last visited the park—in late autumn, when the leaves were fallen, the waters turning frigid. I've thrived on the solitude at Poinsett many a cold day, but this one was bitter. I suppose the memory of it was the main reason it had been six and a half years.

The Fourth of July is an apt time to visit, for the High Hills of the Santee were dearly loved by Revolutionary War hero Thomas Sumter and other notables of American history. It was the one day of summer I had available for a magazine photo shoot. My nine-year-old niece Maddie wanted to tag along and help me take pictures.

The park had changed considerably. It was greener and more lush than I ever remembered it, even in summer. Trees completely obstructed the view of the lake from the overlook shelter. Overall, though, it was the same as always. The primordial smell of a moss-stony creek. Bombardments by mischievous squirrels armed with acorns and nuts. Huge fallen, rotting logs. The strange coquina foundations and the silent, moss-draped cabin village.

I rented one of the cabins with my daughter Courtney about 1992, when she was a kid. She wasn't as enamored with Poinsett as I, but she took along lots of reading and was happy to relax. Courtney has fond memories of it today. I suspect it was rather like annual family beach vacations. Children secretly enjoy swimming and crabbing and exploring, but mainly what they talk about while they're there is how bored they are. Then as adults, all they remember are the fun moments, and they yearn for those long-ago experiences.

As for Maddie, she quickly found herself swatting at bugs. (Do take repellant if you visit in the warm months.) I was oblivious to the bites; perhaps I've become immune.

Notwithstanding the annoyance, Maddie never once whined about going home the two hours we were there—significant, I believe. It suggests children at an early age perceive something very different and appealing about this place—something they just might return to and embrace for many years to come.

Poinsett would be my absolute perfect getaway but for the absence of some local haunting or mystery to be pondered at a cabin fireside on a blustery winter evening. "The Vanishing Horseman of the Heights," or "The Bride Who Weeps at Midnight," or "The Decapitated Logger."

I can invent one.

Next trip . . . . ☽

☽

Solace Among the Sycamores

Where are they? Where are all the people who should be out here at the West Columbia Riverwalk? After all, it's a gorgeous late summer afternoon, and the temperature has mercifully dipped below ninety degrees. It's about ten degrees cooler in the shade, so thanks to the canopy of trees covering most of this park, I'm thoroughly enjoying my walk along the lighted pathways and boardwalks that offer breathtaking views of the Congaree River. I almost have the whole place to myself though, and I wonder why.

Perhaps people don't realize it is an oasis of natural beauty amidst the congestion of Columbia's Vista district and West Columbia's urban center. Great blue herons, Canada geese, snowy white egrets and other beautiful birds perch on granite boulders that dot the Congaree. That bird nesting near the top of that pine tree might even be an American bald eagle.

The trees are just as magnificent as the wildlife they nurture. Sweet gums. River birches. Southern magnolias. Turkey oaks. And the sycamores. Oh, the sycamores. They amaze me most of all. As they stretch skyward, they shed their bark, revealing limbs that look like they were intricately carved from alabaster. It is as if they are growing out of themselves and by doing so, they show me how to do the same, how to shed old habits and ways of thinking that no longer serve me. These are ancient, wise trees, and each of them has a soul—I'm sure of it. Like humans, each of them is unique, and like all living beings, they are constantly changing as they journey from beginning of life to its end.

The river is ever-changing too. It never looks exactly the same from one day to the next. Depending on a variety of factors, including the intensity of sunlight, the water appears blue, then gray, then brown, and then a range of shades between. Sometimes this merging of the Saluda and Broad rivers

Sandra E. Johnson on the West Columbia side of the Congaree Riverwalk.
Photograph by Lynne Branham.

forms a raw, wild torrent; sometimes it's almost as tranquil and still as a
pond. Sometimes it reveals hundreds of rocks and boulders; sometimes it
nearly hides them.

Too many people are missing out on this. They don't even know it exists.
Neither did I until a friend told me about it around six years ago. But, since
then, I've been trying to spread the word about what a jewel it is. With its

benches, picnic tables and covered shelters, it makes a perfect destination for family picnics, romantic dates, or simply having quiet time alone. And why slog away on boring treadmills, stationary bikes and Stairmasters when there are these wonderful trails to walk, jog or bike on? They make even the most challenging workout regime more enjoyable.

The park offers a lot of interesting information about the area's history, too. Exhibits placed along walkways tell how the cities bordering the Congaree, including the state's capital, started as small colonial settlements. They narrate how the river was the region's main economic artery during eras in which the only way to move large amounts of commercial goods was by boats and barges. A reproduction of a typical river inn is one more thing that sparks imaginings of what life must have been like here hundreds of years ago.

This place—timeless yet constantly evolving. Each moment here is a reminder that everything is in the process of being created, existing, then dissolving; and recognition of this softens the sharp edges of my pain over the unexpected death of my forty-seven-year-old brother and other losses. Yes, this place is a source of solace. No manmade structure, not even the most beautiful of cathedrals, could give me what this place does because despite all our knowledge and skills, we humans cannot create nature. We can only be a small part of it. So I keep walking through the park and drawing sustenance from it, and as I feel a breeze from the river, inhale the fragrance from honeysuckle, and hear the chirping of mating cardinals, my problems lessen and my head clears. And I am reminded that life is truly good. ☽

Reflection in the Water

Anyone who has ever worked for a newspaper knows the "controlled chaos" that goes on before deadline. Some nights you literally hold your breath and hope no computer glitches slow you down. After deadline, everyone heads out the door and either stops by a late-night watering hole or goes home to watch TV or read. It generally takes an hour or so to release the stress.

Once, after an especially bad night at *The Beaufort Gazette* when we barely made deadline because of a late-breaking story, I decided I needed to go somewhere quiet. I had already discovered the Port Royal Boardwalk Park—known locally as "The Sands"—and I knew it could bring my heart rate down.

I strolled along the lengthy boardwalk, listening as a fish jumped out of the water and splashed. I tried to see it, but on this moonless night all I could see was the blackness of Batter Creek at Port Royal Sound. Perhaps halfway toward the end, I sat down and performed my usual routine of closing my eyes and inhaling deeply, reveling in the briny saltwater smell. As I slowly exhaled, the magic of the Sands at night enveloped me. I opened my eyes and found myself staring into a sky dotted with millions, if not billions, of pinpoints of light, many twinkling against the ebony space. Never had I seen so many stars. Here were the Big Dipper, the Little Dipper, and even Orion. Unlike the textbook photos from college astronomy, each constellation was bathed in a wash of dimmer stars. I was spellbound.

Besides the sandy beach area, the Sands has a floating dock, a boat ramp and a boardwalk. Actually, "boardwalk" is a misnomer. It's actually 1,250 feet of cement slabs resting on a wooden frame, which makes walking easier. It winds along the waterfront, only a few feet above the high tide mark, providing views of the water, surrounding marsh and protected oyster beds

Kendall Bell on the Sands boardwalk.
Photograph by Bob Sofaly.

beneath the structure. From a four-story observation tower, you can get a panoramic look at the intersection of Battery Creek and the Beaufort River from the Russell Bell Bridge (S.C. Highway 802) to Port Royal Sound at the mouth of the Atlantic Ocean. Across the river is the Marine Corps Recruit Depot Parris Island.

Breathtaking at night, the Sands is entertaining by day. It's not unusual to see bottle-nosed dolphins, raccoons, and numerous species of birds. One day, a dolphin spied me on the dock. It swam almost to the edge of the boardwalk and blew me a "whoosh" of greeting. As soon as I leaned forward for a better view, it disappeared, but not before I stole a good look at it.

Every July Fourth, boaters come to watch fireworks that burst first from the Town of Port Royal, then Parris Island, and finally in the distance, Hilton Head Island. With some friends on a boat, we packed a cooler and cast off from the Beaufort Downtown Marina, dropping anchor after a two-to-three-mile ride. Darkness fell. Soon, the boats were crowded so close it seemed I could have stepped completely across Port Royal Sound from boat to boat without ever getting wet. The people on our left offered beer, wine and lots of food. We likewise shared our picnic. Soon, people were passing food and drinks between the boats as if it were a family reunion.

At 9 P.M., several people tuned their radios to a station playing patriotic music. Suddenly, we heard a loud "Boom!" Red fireworks shot skyward, exploding into a multicolored starburst. The reflection drizzled upon the water, and the crowd oohed and ahhed after every thundering crack. When Port Royal's fireworks ended, Parris Island's began. Then off in the distance, we saw Hilton Head's fireworks light the sky. Meanwhile, every patriotic song I think I have ever heard was broadcast across the water from several boats. Then suddenly, the night got quiet. Sandi Patty began singing the National Anthem, and chills shot down my arms. I thanked God for the brave men and women in our armed forces. And I thought about my own father, a disabled veteran from World War II, who never got to enjoy a normal life because of his injuries.

Dad never revealed the details of his time in the Army. When he was asked how he got injured, his usual response was, "it was just war. And things like that happen during war." After he died in 1987, I found copies of military records that showed he was guarding the munitions storage area at Fort Sill, Oklahoma, when several other soldiers horsing around accidentally pulled the pin from a hand grenade. The panicking soldier hurled it as far as he could. The grenade landed in the doorway of the munitions storage area, causing a huge explosion. Dad was burned from the waist up, his vocal cords severed.

At first, it didn't appear he would survive. Later, doctors somehow repaired his vocal cords but his speech was never the same. While our family could understand him, he often had to repeat himself. Or a family member explained to others what he had said. Dad survived a lot, but after being diagnosed with Parkinson's disease and later suffering a heart attack and several strokes, he died two weeks shy of spending eighteen months in the William Jennings Bryan Dorn V.A. Hospital in Columbia. I had never felt so proud of being an American when I realized everything he had endured. And yes, on that hot Fourth of July night, I had a lump in my throat and tears in my eyes listening to Sandi Patty sing.

My newspaper days are behind me now. But I remember the stress of those deadlines and the relief I found near the waters of Port Royal. When I look into those waters, I see a middle-aged man, shrouded with thinning gray hair. The face is much like my father's. I close my eyes, lick the salty brine from my lips, and listen to a dolphin playing nearby. Yes, Dad would have loved the Sands. ◝

Photo courtesy of Clemson University
Sports Information Department.

From the Press Box

"I am not in favor of adding a sport where you sit on your ass and go backwards."

Clemson football coach and director of athletics Frank Howard (1909–1996), when asked about the possibility of a college rowing team

Where Dreams Rise and Fall

A cool sea breeze sweeps in off the Ashley River, flapping the flags that stand tall in centerfield against a pink western sky, giving much-needed relief to the crowd as it slowly fills the seats at Joe Riley Park.

In a city known for its history, culinary delights and hordes of tourists, the best place to experience the real Charleston is sitting somewhere down the first base line at the Joe. Named in honor of the Holy City's long-time

America's pastime at Charleston's leveling field, the Joseph P. Riley Jr. Park. Photograph by Andy Solomon.

mayor, this jewel of a baseball park is laid in the pluff mud like an abandoned shrimp boat that washed up during a bad storm.

From almost any vantage point I can see the confluence of two great rivers, the Ashley and the Cooper, as they merge to form the Atlantic Ocean. Just by walking into the stadium seats, green and curved perfectly around the field, I can smell the ocean's pungent perfume and hear the fiddler crabs as they scurry among the spartina grasses at low tide. As I look westward, toward the suburbs, the sky darkens as a summer thunderstorm threatens, painting over the last blushing rays of a day with deep purple clouds destined to ruin someone else's evening.

To the left, church steeples grace the skyline of the peninsula, and between innings I can hear the mournful sound of a bugler ending another long day for cadets at the Citadel.

For all the attention Charleston gets for being a vacation destination for the well-heeled traveler, a haven for restaurant savants, a magnet for sun worshipers, and the place novelist Pat Conroy drools over, it is, above all that, a great place for ordinary people to live. The reasons are simple—lots of water and southern hospitality.

South Carolina has seen more than a million visitors turn into residents in the past few decades, and most of them have burrowed into the crab holes somewhere along our sandy coastline. Though we used to call them Yankees, we have softened our language to simply say they're from "off," a designation they understand and accept. Especially when they get to know the natives and how deep the pride and love of the Lowcountry runs through generations of South Carolinians.

When I was growing up in Allendale, some eighty miles from anywhere, people from New York, New Jersey, Pennsylvania, and Ohio were transients who spent a necessary night in our mom-and-pop motels along U.S. Highway 301 en route to Florida. That was before Interstate 95 was carved through the Pee Dee and down the neck of the nothingness to make their time spent in the Palmetto State even shorter. Few, if any, ever thought of staying very long. There were gnats, and mosquitoes, and nasty little boogers called no-see-ums that kept them moving toward Miami, Daytona, and Fort Lauderdale.

But there came a time—the exact month and day is not recorded, but it was like a tidal shift from low to high—when all these tourists suddenly discovered Hilton Head Island. From there they spread like kudzu up the coast and inland to towns like Summerville and Conway where they stayed, for better or for worse.

The author at the Joe.
Photograph by G. David Gentry.

That's why it feels so good to be in Section 204 at the Joe. It's far from the chicken-wire ball yards I knew as a country boy. Back then the bleachers were sunbaked 2x4s with nails half-hammered and folded over. There was always pigeon poop on the seats and a strong scent of ammonia. Baseball was played in temporary temples, and nobody thought much about how they looked, or what they smelled like. They just were.

I actually preferred a field a few miles out of town, where the black boys played on Sunday afternoons. The base paths were actually rutted with season after season of hard-nosed ball, and the outfield fence was made of rusty car hoods. Nothing fancy, but it sizzled with excitement. That's where I learned black people have more fun than white people. Whether it's in church or on the baseball field, they get involved, emotionally, physically, and spiritually.

That's the way I saw baseball for most of my life in South Carolina—black and white. And then it changed.

Sometimes you have to be sitting right next to something to see it clearly. For me it was a hot summer's night at the Joe when I was a sportswriter looking for a sidebar. With permission from the manager, I spent the game in the RiverDogs' dugout, talking with the players. What I learned was they have the worst seat in the house, but the most interesting. That's because baseball represents a sea change in America. In order to play baseball at this level, you must speak Spanish. Or at least some baseball Spanish.

How to tell a teammate he did good. How to tell the ump to go to hell. The basics.

That's when I realized this group of young players looked a lot like the audience. A melting pot in short sleeves, flip flops, faded College of Charleston T-shirts. Many are military with haircuts high and tight, toting hot dogs and cold drinks for their young families. The game they see is different from the one viewed from the dugout where major league wannabes practice spitting and other baseball behavior.

But while they're aspiring to be in Yankee Stadium, they provide the Holy City with a perfect backdrop for family entertainment. Here in a scale model of Baltimore's cavernous Camden Yards, dreams rise and fall on the crack of a bat, the roar of the crowd, the oohs and aahs that follow a close play at second base. It's almost, but not quite, as exciting as the zany promotions that entertain the crowd between innings.

There are the ubiquitous sumo wrestlers dressed in puffy outfits who run into each other and bounce off like flubber; the hot dog twins, one dressed as a bun, the other as a wiener, as they try to come together as one. Not a moment is wasted, much to the delight of the crowd that sips beer and talks about the weather, politics, and the news of the day to the casual cadence of minor league baseball.

And not a speck of pigeon poop anywhere.

Charleston, for a small city, is blessed with beautiful, modern sporting venues that larger towns could envy. This gem along the riverfront is part of a set that includes the North Charleston Coliseum where the Stingrays play pro hockey, Blackbaud Stadium on Daniel Island where the Charleston Battery plays professional soccer; the Family Circle tennis facility where Venus and Serena appear; Carolina First Arena, a beautiful basketball facility tucked neatly into the webwork of buildings on Meeting Street where the College of Charleston Cougars play basketball; and Johnson Hagood Stadium, the fortress-like football stadium where the Citadel Bulldogs do battle on autumn afternoons. The only problem with Charleston is there is all too often too much to do.

From the art galleries to the internationally acclaimed restaurants to the Market to King Street's antique stores to the Battery to Fort Sumter to the beaches to an evening strolling the cobblestone streets and peeking through windows of historic homes, this is a city of opportunity and romance that draws millions of visitors who all leave with secret dreams of returning someday to live.

But it was not always thus.

The Charleston I love today is not the Charleston I knew as a child of the south. Back then it was a gray, worn-out relic of a lost cause that sat for a century in mothballs while other southern cities stripped away the remnants of defeat and built asphalt parking lots and box-like office buildings. Charleston, broke and beleaguered by the Civil War, simply sat in a pool of pity and stagnated in its indignity. By the 1960s, she looked like an aging stripper without a backup plan.

The renaissance began in the late 1970s with the vision of Mayor Joe Riley and others who understood that what was left was worth its weight in real estate gold. First came the hotels, then the restaurants, then the golf courses, then the preservation of the past, renewed interest in the plantations, and a diversified economy. Add a lot of money and a beautiful new bridge across the Cooper River to the yuppie suburb of Mount Pleasant and the sea islands and the ever-expanding neighborhoods where blue herons and egrets still grace the landscape in almost every direction, and you have the recipe that made us what we are today—perhaps the best city in the world to live and play and take in a ballgame when the RiverDogs are in town. ☽

When Camelot Came to Columbia

As a newspaper sports editor in Savannah in the 1960s I was keenly aware of the University of South Carolina's athletic endeavors because a significant portion of our readership was interested. So we covered the Gamecocks on a regular basis, albeit with not much enthusiasm, I'm afraid—except during basketball season, and then only because of their membership in the Atlantic Coast Conference. Then, as now, the ACC was regularly the home of some of the best college basketball programs in the country; unfortunately, USC was never among them. That all began to change when Frank McGuire came to town in 1964.

So it was that my ultimate love affair with USC basketball sprang from nebulous and tangential beginnings. As George Bailey learned, one man's life touches so many others. For me, that man was McGuire. It began as I fed quarters into a coin-operated television (an early version of "pay TV") in a motel near Charlotte on a cold March night in 1957. I was sixteen at the time and returning from a family trip with my parents when we chanced to overnight near one of only a handful of TV stations broadcasting the NCAA basketball championship. (The Final Four hoopla we know today was hardly more than a national afterthought in those days.) Kansas and its giant sophomore, Wilt Chamberlain, were favored against McGuire's North Carolina squad, and the savvy Irishman surprised everyone by sending out his smallest player for the opening center jump against Chamberlain, then triple-teamed him the rest of the night. The result was a 54–53 triple over-time win for the Tar Heels, and I was forever after a diehard McGuire fan— as was Wilt Chamberlain. The pair teamed up for one year in the NBA, and Chamberlain always proclaimed him the best coach he ever played for.

Tom Riker, Rick Aydlett, Bob Carver, John Roche, Assistant Coach Buck
Freeman, Coach Frank McGuire, Assistants Donnie Walsh and Bill Loving.
Photograph by Billy Deal.

When McGuire signed on to coach the Gamecocks in 1964, it signaled
the beginning of what would soon become, at least for me, the most exciting period in the history of South Carolina sports. McGuire was head
coach for sixteen years and the first two were his only losing seasons. Fans
got a tantalizing glimpse of the good things to come during McGuire's
second year in Columbia, when the Gamecocks upset third-ranked Duke
in the old USC Field House, a tiny gym that looked like something out of
Hoosiers. Two years later, on Nov. 30, 1968, Camelot opened in Columbia
when McGuire's squad christened still-unfinished Carolina Coliseum with
a 51–49 win over Auburn.

That date also marked the debut of John Roche, a lanky sophomore
guard who, along with McGuire, would define college basketball for that
generation of South Carolinians. It was in Roche's junior year that USC
reached the pinnacle of its basketball fortunes with a season record of 24–3,
made even sweeter by an undefeated conference slate. But, alas, Ed Left-
wich, a name that will live in infamy, stamped *fini* to the Gamecock season when he stole a pass and put the final points on a most improbable
N.C. State upset in the ACC finals. In those days, only the winner of the

conference tournament was allowed to advance to the NCAAs, and because USC was hosting a regional it wasn't even allowed to compete in the lesser National Invitation Tournament, creating the most egregious double whammy in recorded history.

So by the time I arrived in Columbia in the summer of 1970, Carolina was well established as a perennial powerhouse. For the next ten years, through the end of McGuire's tenure at USC, I sat cross-legged beneath the baskets in Carolina Coliseum and photographed every home game but one (Duquesne, 1977), as Roche, Tom Owens, Kevin Joyce, Tom Riker, Alex English, Mike Dunleavy, Brian Winters, Nate Davis, Jackie Gilloon, Mike Doyle, Zam Fredrick and dozens of others frolicked before me and appreciative, sold-out crowds. I have not attended a USC basketball game since 1980, but even now, thirty years later, every time I ride by the grand old pile that is Carolina Coliseum, nostalgia nudges me with memories as fresh as a carnation in Frank McGuire's lapel.

The Coliseum, with a seating capacity of 12,401, was USC's home court until 2002, when operations moved to the Colonial Center, half a mile and a lifetime away. The opening night crowd that saw Carolina nip Auburn in 1968 was the largest to witness a basketball game in South Carolina to that point. The tan and red rubberlike floor was a thing of beauty, but the lighting was so centric that when a player dribbled into the corner I had to adjust my camera exposure by at least two stops to account for the falloff. In the early 1970s, WIS-TV televised every home game, and on every foul shot two guys would roll a huge camera and tripod under the basket to get a close-up of the shooter, so photographers had to move camera bags and make sure toes and fingers were out of danger. Portability had not yet consumed our lives with cell phones, laptops and video shoulder cams. It was funny because by the time they got the camera in place the player had usually finished his free throws, and the action was headed to the other end. Still, every free throw situation, here came the camera. We photographers had to position ourselves so we were not blocked by the officials or worse, cheerleaders.

Attending a game in Carolina Coliseum was unique. It was large enough to have the full trappings of a major college game, yet more intimate and manageable than today's giant houses. The pep band that was a fixture in the corner by the visitors' bench generated the decibel level of a full marching unit when the Gamecocks were on a tear, and a congenial mix of students and other fans kept things loud but never rowdy. Every game was a sellout in the early days of the decade. It was an atmosphere reminiscent of

John Roche com-
manding the court.
Photograph by Billy
Deal.

below: Carolina
Coliseum, 1969
(University Archives).
Courtesy of South
Caroliniana Library,
University of South
Carolina, Columbia.

a huge family reunion, or the first day of a county fair, and Gene McKay's soothing baritone came loud and clear over the public address system. Press row was directly floor side, and there was seldom a game without at least one player diving headlong into the typewriters and microphones in pursuit of a lost ball. Fans would walk slowly as they passed behind the working media, hoping to hear a snippet of Bob Fulton's crisp description of another Tom Owens rebound.

In fifty years of covering sports I have photographed Joe Namath, Hank Aaron, Jerry West, and Johnny Unitas, and I can truthfully say I never enjoyed watching any of them play more than John Roche, a two-time All-America and two-time Atlantic Coast Conference MVP. That may sound a bit provincial (I was a little eccentric in the '70s), but all those winter afternoons and nights, sitting on that Coliseum floor watching Roche completely control a basketball game, were the most enjoyable of my career. In those days the Gamecocks played a deliberate, slow-paced game (there was no shot clock), and my most vivid memory is watching Roche walk the ball up the floor, in defiant command, daring and staring down the opposing players—and coaches. In 1971, when bitter rivalry between the Gamecocks and Tar Heels escalated to open hatred, UNC Coach Dean Smith mildly chastised Roche and his mates for overly aggressive play. In the first half of USC's 72–66 win, Roche was bringing the ball upcourt when he stopped momentarily in front of the opposing bench and said something to Smith before continuing his dribble. Smith seemed bemused but didn't respond. When asked later what Roche had said, Smith sheepishly repeated what can only be described as the all-time favorite expression of army sergeants, movie gangsters, and Richard Pryor.

McGuire's New York roots and his early years at St. John's University produced numerous contacts in the region, and he recruited heavily in the New York/New Jersey area. His players were the apotheosis of street-smart, rough-and-tumble city kids, and McGuire set the tone with his iron-fist-in-the-velvet-glove routine. His dapper dress and quiet manner belied his tough-guy approach to the game, and his players were all too willing to act as enforcers. The physical style of play was actually a major factor in USC's eventual withdrawal from the ACC. Bitter battles with the conference over the eligibility of prize recruit Mike Grosso, aggravated by the intense rivalry with the North Carolina schools, led to irreconcilable differences. USC's ultimate departure in 1971, soon after Paul Dietzel's arrival as athletics director, seemed an inevitable conclusion.

One of the most memorable, and regrettable, moments in Coliseum history occurred when Maryland, coached by Lefty Driesell, came to town in 1970. Trying to break up a scuffle among the players, Driesell was clocked by a roundhouse right by John Ribock—a tough guy not from New York but Augusta, Georgia. After fits of fuming and threats of lawsuits, Lefty calmed down and struck a blow of his own: "I've been hit harder," he sneered. Marquette's Bob Lackey was the victim the following year when Tom Riker landed an unexpected haymaker, resulting in one of the all-time great quotes from a visiting player: "That dude sucker-punched me!"

Although McGuire didn't have a losing season during the '70s, the first half of the decade was where the stars lived, and the Gamecocks won at least twenty games every year from 1969 to 1974. Kevin Joyce was close to Roche in talent if not charisma. In 1972, his three NCAA titles still ahead of him, Bobby Knight brought his Indiana team to the Coliseum. Although it was only Knight's second year at the helm, the Hoosiers were already establishing themselves as title contenders and would indeed reach the Final Four that season. They started strong and built a 17-point lead in the second half. Then Joyce proved he belonged in the pantheon of Gamecock icons. He scored his jersey number (43) to push USC to an 88–85 win. It was one of the best individual performances I ever saw in that hallowed hall.

So now the Domed Lady hosts job fairs, serves as a rehearsal venue for rock concerts, and houses academic units, awaiting either refurbishment or demolition. But on those winter nights when she's dark and quiet, and the air is cold and the wind is right, the cheers are sometimes audible from the bigger, newer place half a mile away, evoking the time when Marilyn Monroe returned from entertaining servicemen in Korea. Still glowing from her enthusiastic reception by the troops, she said to her husband, "Oh, Joe, you never heard such cheering!" "Yes," said Joe DiMaggio quietly, "I have." ⟩

Photo courtesy of the State Archives of Florida.

Becoming and Overcoming

"There is a place in God's sun for the youth 'farthest down' who has the vision, the determination, and the courage to reach it."

Mayesville native Mary McLeod Bethune (1875-1955), who organized the National Council of Negro Women, advised President Franklin D. Roosevelt, and established a school for girls in Florida that later became Bethune-Cookman College.

Robin Asbury Cutler

The Musty Smell of Books

My favorite place now lives in the clutter of childhood memories, images flickering in early morning dreams brought on by the distant sound of a train whistle. Yes, the train's engineer has no idea that the whistle he blows binds me to another train passing through Connie Maxwell Children's Home in Greenwood more than forty years before. The tracks were removed long ago, possibly to stem the tide of runaways looking for adventure, freedom, and the only ticket home. My little brother was often among those hitching a ride.

Lest you worry this is not a happy tale, let me assure you that all ends well, or at least well enough for me. That train never carried me away, but its whistle did offer me comfort as a seven-year-old girl being dropped off on a cold March day, 1961, at the girls cottage, White-Morehead. My Uncle Bob, a Southern Baptist preacher, had prayed to Jesus to take care of me and my siblings after my grandmother's death, father's stroke, parents' divorce, and subsequent breakdown of the family. As luck would have it, Uncle Bob and Jesus worked things out because Connie Maxwell became my home for the next six years. Prayer is a powerful thing.

Uncle Bob delivered me to the back porch of the cottage and into the hands of Mrs. Lynch, my new surrogate mother. She was a childless widow with a droopy left eye and cropped gray hair who wasted no time teaching me her favorite lesson: that godliness and cleanliness are intertwined. On that fateful day, I was brave like Uncle Bob said Jesus wanted me to be and let the old woman pull me weeping from the back seat of his car. Mrs. Lynch put her cold hands on my shoulders to help calm me down as we watched Uncle Bob's station wagon slowly drive away.

Overnight, a mop and bucket replaced my dolls and toys; the New Testament supplanted my beloved *Arabian Nights*. I would learn that Mrs. Lynch was widely regarded as the most strict cottage mother on campus. She didn't favor the usual trappings of childhood like television, toys, bicycles, and radios although she did allow us to watch *Bonanza* on Sunday nights because she had a fondness for Ben Cartwright. We would often listen to gospel music on her hi-fi as we drifted off to sleep each night around 8:30. Ferlin Husky's gospel classic, "On the Wings of a Snow White Dove," is permanently etched in my memory.

In the early 1960s, children in first to third grades attended the campus school, a drafty two-story building in the center of campus under the shade of sprawling oak trees. On my first day after sitting all morning trying hard not to be noticed, I trailed behind my classmates out of the building and down a muddy dirt road to the lunchroom. I would find there the only minority person on campus, a friendly black cook named Janie who served up steaming pots of fresh vegetables from the campus farm along with buttered biscuits and cornbread. As I would discover, our lunches often included slices of her fruit pies topped with homemade ice cream. The food at Connie Maxwell was plentiful, homegrown, and cooked southern style.

Within days of getting settled into school, my teacher, Mrs. Timmerman, realized I was an exceptional reader. In no time she was making me stand up to read aloud in class. This did nothing but make me a red-hot target for bullying. Mrs. Timmerman nearly yanked the ears off a boy when she caught him strapping me to the basketball goal after school a few days later. Sprinting across the outdoor track she yelled that she would paddle him within an inch of his life if he ever touched me again. She grabbed up the heap I had become, wiped my tears with her long, coarse skirt, and pulled me into a small building directly across from the school.

This was the campus library and it would become my favorite place in the world, then and now. It was a small house with a heavy wooden door that creaked like the doors in horror movies.

Once we entered the vestibule, I saw the room was arranged with wooden shelves stacked to the ceiling with a treasure of books. Across from the stacks was a desk topped with a small drawer containing the catalog of the library's collection and carefully penciled patron cards. Behind the desk stood a large table with mismatched chairs piled with old magazines and newspapers. A smaller table was pushed under two corner windows that afforded natural light even on cloudy days. Here Mrs. Timmerman would do her art projects, paint dishes, and make dolls out of yarn and clothespins.

The E. P. McKissick Library, (1905–1970) at Connie Maxwell Children's Home.
Drawing by Connie Maxwell alumni Mack Baltzegar, courtesy of
Connie Maxwell Children's Home.

Mrs. Timmerman was roundly feared by most of the children on campus because she was peculiar looking, very tall and thin with a purposeful walk. Except for the red hair that sat on top of her head like steel wool, she looked much like Elvira Gulch, the Wicked Witch from *The Wizard of Oz*. She would regularly paddle students caught talking behind her back or passing notes as she chalked math problems on the blackboard. Many unfortunate children who couldn't trace perfect letters on their practice sheets had their palms struck three times with a wooden ruler.

But for some reason, Mrs. Timmerman had a soft spot for me. Maybe it was my red hair or how I was relentlessly picked on by the other students. Whatever the reason, the woman and the library made a profound difference to me at a time when I needed someone to notice and care. Whenever I passed through those creaky library doors, I would be ensconced in the world of books and art that would become the foundation for the rest of my life. Just as Dorothy was suddenly cast into a world of brilliant color after being blown from the barren Kansas landscape, my destiny was just as quickly and mysteriously changed.

My benefactress somehow convinced Mrs. Lynch that I should be relieved of mopping and dusting to help in the library after school. I would sometimes push a broom around and reshelve books, but mainly I sat at that table under the windows and read books and magazines quietly passing the time. Mrs. Timmerman rarely spoke to me except to correct my art projects or to tell me I had shelved a book in the wrong place. I learned to treasure silence.

During the six years I lived at Connie Maxwell, I think I read every book in that library. My favorites were classics like *Wuthering Heights, Jane Eyre,* and the Jane Austens. But I especially loved the more modern Nancy Drew series. The girl detective was spunky and often found herself in desperate situations. I remember she was once trapped in an attic that reminded me of a time when Mrs. Lynch locked me in the cottage attic for punishment. Unlike Nancy, I wasn't able to escape through a window but had to wait until the old woman released me. I couldn't compare my life to the Hardy Boys mysteries but read that series undercover since Mrs. Timmerman thought it wasn't appropriate literature for girls.

As the months turned into years, the church would become the second-most important place for me outside the library. With my strong alto voice, I joined the choir under the direction of Mrs. Chipley, a devoted retired woman from town who gamely sacrificed her time and patience to teach us to sing the repertoire of the Southern Baptist hymnal. Mrs. Chipley had a curious nervous tick: she would purse her lips precisely ten times followed by a wide yawn followed again by ten pursed lips. When she would move from her perch at the organ to the front pew in the choir loft to listen to the sermon, we would mock her yawn and throw tiny spitballs rolled from the torn corners of the hymnals at her teased, lacquered silver hair. She would gingerly pick out the wads and look so sad and hurt that we gave up the abuse in short order.

In my second year on campus, I was called to the office to meet with my counselor, Miss Johnson. She explained that the women's Sunday school class at the First Baptist Church in Greenville was looking for a girl to sponsor and they had selected me from school pictures they had seen. Miss Johnson said they liked that I had a face "covered with freckles" and that I looked "happy." I was put on a bus alone for the trip to Greenville, where my sponsors met me for a weekend of shopping and fun. Each October, they would buy me dresses, play clothes, coats, and sweaters. In the spring, I would return and shop for my Easter dress, summer clothes, underwear and shoes. My pilgrimage to Greenville would repeat itself like clockwork through the years and I still have a warm spot for that city and those women. They elevated my station in life by transforming me from a ragged little orphan to one of the best-dressed students in all of Greenwood. I am forever in debt to the First Baptist Church of Greenville.

My cottage also was adopted by a fraternity from Clemson University whose members would come and give us a Christmas party each year. Looking back I'm not sure why it was allowed for a group of young men to associate with young, impressionable girls, but the party they would throw was the most anticipated event of the year. The boys were handsome and rambunctious while being perfect gentlemen. We all fell in love with them to various degrees, including Mrs. Lynch. They would flirt with her and she would blush and laugh as she drank their Cokes, ate their cookies and potato chips—treats that were never part of our regular diet. The party was the only time I remember Mrs. Lynch looking like a real person and it was the rare time she allowed us into the living room. To be able to sit on the forbidden vinyl furniture and to see Mrs. Lynch actually laugh made me realize that all things are subject to change.

Mrs. Lynch was not at the cottage one afternoon as we got off the school bus. Our substitute cottage mother explained that Mrs. Lynch had been taken to the hospital with chest pains. She had not been herself since the Kennedy assassination and had never fully recovered from the grief she felt watching Jackie walk behind those horses pulling the flag-draped coffin. Mrs. Lynch often wept openly and was inconsolable in the months that followed. She never returned to White-Morehead Cottage and disappeared forever from my life, just as quickly and completely as the witch from Oz melted away after being hit with the bucket of water.

And like the flying monkeys post-witch, the girls in the cottage started experiencing more freedom. Now we could accept sleepover invitations from school friends, watch TV, go away to summer camp, talk to boys at church, polish our fingernails. My siblings started visiting me and I could have toys and books in my room. I treasured a red transistor radio that my Uncle Ray sent me from New Mexico. It introduced me to '60s rock n' roll music and world news. At ten, I fell in love with Paul McCartney. At twelve, I switched to Davy Jones of the Monkees.

Just before I was to start eighth grade at Southside Junior High, I left Connie Maxwell as suddenly as I had appeared six years earlier. My mother pulled up to the back porch in her white Plymouth Valiant and told me to go pack my clothes; I was going home to Charleston. My brother had jumped his last train and Jesus had spoken to the campus administrators that it was time for him to go. I didn't get to say goodbye to my school friends or to become a cheerleader after being elected to the school squad at the end of the term. Still, I eagerly climbed into the back seat with my brother and we happily drove home with our mother.

As I look back on those childhood years through adult eyes, I see there were tragic parts that echo *Oliver Twist*. But, in my memory, Connie Maxwell more resembled Peter Pan's Neverland in that it was inhabited by children who grew up with little adult influence. I became self-reliant at an early age and my survival instincts are still well-honed. My love of books and the arts were both nourished to shape who I would become and the profession I would choose. The musty smell of old books still floods me with feelings of security and warmth. I love organ music, singing from a hymnal, and going to church on Sundays although I eventually discovered my spiritual home was with the Unitarians. Certainly, I would not be the person I am today without the years I lived in Greenwood.

I rejoice that the sound of a passing train can take me there anytime I please. ☽

Dianne "Dinah" Johnson

)

The Beautiful Ugly

A black female doctor delivered me in Charleston, South Carolina in 1960. This fact inspires me and pulls me back. Summer after summer, I roam the streets for hours, letting the sun have its way, bronzing me, browning me more deeply.

Everything here is beautiful, I lie to myself.

The voice of my graduate school professor echoes in my head. Cultural contact is not just one-way. Southern hospitality. African hospitality. One and the same. When I go to the beach, I listen across the water, hoping to hear the voices of my family across the sea. Of a little black girl like me.

In Charleston, I walk through gorgeous wrought-iron gates born of the genius and generous spirit of Mr. Philip Simmons and I make myself at home, in Charleston. This place I love. And don't love.

In Holly Hill, South Carolina, the place where both of my parents were born, I belong and don't belong. Children here don't quite know what to make of me and my sisters and brother. We're all right with them only because we're Dickie and Roland Johnson's cousins. But they think we're different and uppity; talking proper (sounding white) is the kiss of death. My shyness is the kiss of death. Sometimes I walk with my sister Debbi and my cousin Kima to her granddaddy's store and he'll give us candy. It's safe to roam the roads of this little southern town, not quite distinguishable from other little southern towns. Except for the houses that are harbors for me. Mostly I stay inside Grandma Frona's house, and no matter where I turn my head, I see photographs of family, in military uniforms, in white shirts for school, in front of the juke box. Mostly, I ask Frona questions and questions and more questions. She doesn't talk just to talk, but filling in the family history is another thing.

My favorite story is about her and church. Lovely Hill Baptist Church in Holly Hill, South Carolina. It's my family church on both sides, going back to the late 1800s. The minister in the late fifties, early sixties felt big and bold enough to insult my Grandmother Frona right from the pulpit, right during service. Her sister Dorothy wasn't going to stand for that. She got up, marched right up to the pulpit, and knocked the preacher out cold. If you were a Cain, somebody always had your back. My forthright, fierce, loyal family. These are the people I come from.

Around the corner from Frona's house is Grandma Clara's house. Grandmama Clara used to live in Boston, and there, in the city, in addition to other work, she was an Avon Lady. Suited her perfectly, my pretty, precious grandmama. Crocheted doilies on the coffee tables and end tables. Pictures of the trinity on the wall—Jesus, Martin Luther King, Jr., and John F. Kennedy. Pretty clothes in the closets—she could look at any outfit, cut a pattern herself, and be wearing a more fabulous version the next day! In another time she would have been a famous designer. Now she was our beautiful, brave Clara. That was enough for her. I want to believe.

Before this white clapboard house was Clara's, it was her mama's. There is nowhere else in the world like my Great-Grandmother Quinnie's place. (When Quinnie left this house for a couple of years, to be with us in Charleston when Daddy went to Vietnam, she'd be at the front door with her gun whenever a male colleague dropped Mama off after coaching their basketball games. No playing when it came to her granddaughter.) When I think of this place, I hear the rain dancing on the corrugated metal roof, us bundled on the high-built bed, covered with hand-stitched quilts that will stay in our family forever. But, if you go visiting, you'll know it is Quinnie's house (and you'll never forget this house) because before you get up the stairs, there on the middle one, her name is written half an inch deep right into the concrete.

And there's the porch, the best place in the whole wide world. That's where Grandmama Quinnie sat in her wooden rocking chair smoking her pipe. Oh, how I love the smell of tobacco. We'd braid her long yellow-gray hair as she told us about her son John. He went hunting one morning early and didn't make it back alive; a bullet ricocheted off of a tree and shot him. He bled to death, but didn't let that keep him away from his Mama. He used to visit her regular. He'd sit and talk awhile, then tell his Mama he had

The author with her mother, Beatrice Taylor Johnson, and daughter, Niani Feelings, on Quinnie's porch in Holly Hill. Photograph by Robin Price Jumper.

to get back to the graveyard or he'd be barred forever. *Okay Son, I'll see you next time.*

Another time and place and I'll tell you more of Grandma Quinnie's stories. But, now you know, this porch I love. A favorite photo of my own little girl was taken right on these steps, bordered by roses colored coral, in full bloom. (They didn't bloom at all the spring that Clara died.)

In Holly Hill, my mother's family and my father's family are one. You know what I mean; it's one of those places where everyone is related to everyone else. (One Townsend sister is married to Mama's brother and one to Daddy's brother.) At the reunion on Daddy's side, every Thanksgiving for forty years and counting, we have to look in the master book to visualize how the branches and the leaves grow from the tree.

The reunion is in Santee State Park. For some, Santee is a stop on I-95 on the way to Florida. But for me? It is a place I love. It is a place where the children feel free to wander through the woods, pine needles carpeting their paths. (A little one might pick one up to practice her braiding.) It is a place where the children feel free to go to the bait shop and fish a while at the lake. Or walk in the rain. Or throw a pine cone at his brother's head. Brother love.

We are there for days—Wednesday through Saturday, sometimes Sunday. We fill up at least twenty cabins. Kitchenette, bathroom, two bedrooms, pull-out couch in the living room. The essentials are enough, especially considering Lake Marion is right outside the windows. Counting those staying at the park, staying at kinfolks' houses, and friends along for the fellowship, some years we were talking a couple hundred bodies. I won't give you the entire itinerary. But we usually try to include a taping of at least one elder telling his or her story, a formal meal with a program featuring a speaker, a rap session for the teenagers, a fashion show, a talent show, a family investment club meeting, a business meeting (who hasn't paid dues yet?), a fish fry, and on and on, electric sliding into the night.

For years I was the family photographer. Take a look through the albums and you'll see the faces maturing magically, babies eventually holding their own babies on their laps.

It was at Lovely Hill and then at Mama and Daddy's home on the lake in Santee where we celebrated my own daughter's christening. Niani Sekai. Her daddy's translation: A place in Africa filled with laughter.

Every journey to Santee a baptism. Every journey to Holly Hill a prayer of thanks for my forebears. A prayer of thanks that my parents moved on.

And baby, how they moved on. Daddy did ROTC as a way to help with college. Then he and Mama realized it was the way for them and their children to see the country and to see the world. Both my sisters born in Texas. My brother in Germany. There was South Carolina, North Carolina, California, Virginia. In Iran, nobody cared that we were Black Americans. *African. African.* In Philadelphia, we were enthusiastic as could be to visit the Liberty Bell (my parents were masters at getting us excited about each new homeplace). In the city of brotherly love, a "neighbor" painted NIGGER on the trashcans and a preacher came to say *Welcome to the neighborhood but don't come to my church.*

We got around.

And I got around a little bit too, on my own. First, I got myself to Princeton University. Sometime junior year, I was speaking with the recruiter who had found me at Spring Valley High School in Columbia. He recalled a poem I had read to him back then. Me, I had no memory of this. But I was thankful. My poetry (and my parents' love and a few great teachers) had gotten me to Princeton, and Princeton was about to get me to Africa. Kind of.

Really, it was Mr. Freddie Fox '39, Princeton's Number One supporter. I can't remember the details. But there was some transaction I needed to have done at the local bank, right away, or there would be a major glitch in my trip. All was solved when I presented a note, in his handwriting, saying *She's on her way to Africa today. Freddie Fox.* And I was set. Solid. Confident.

But, there, in the Cote D'Ivoire, I am helpless in a market, an old man trying with every language he knows to make me understand him. Finally, someone translates the only question he has at that point. *Where are you from, you lost child?* The only thing that is important to me is that he still considers me a child of Africa. His words make me at home.

I am reborn on the beaches of Bassam. A place in Africa filled with laughter.

To celebrate my fiftieth birthday, I will return to the place of my birth, to Charleston, with my mother and my daughter. In Charleston, we'll walk the cobblestone streets. We'll pass the old auction houses. We'll talk. I'll tell them about a little boy I met in Africa. Upon finding out that I was from the United States, all he could say was *So you are a slave.* That's where his history lesson stopped. I tell him my home is beautiful ugly. That I will go back. Mama and Niani and I will roam the streets for hours, letting the sun have its way, bronzing us, browning us more deeply. We will stand on the Battery and look out across the waters, sending love to our family across the sea.

We are home. ☽

Transformation

It may sound strange that I, a self-proclaimed mama's boy, have chosen the Citadel campus as my place of eternal bliss—a place of refuge, a place of contentment, a place to recharge my batteries when life has sapped me of all my strength. This was the place where lean and tall young men—whose shoes were spit-shined and whose brass belt buckles could blind you—screamed at me, the "fat load" as I ran or did pushups. They swore I'd never finish, but in the end, I graduated a Citadel man.

I chose the Citadel because she chose me as one of her sons. I selected her not because of who I was, but rather because of who I was not. In high school, I was not an athlete, nor was I a particularly good scholar. I, like many, floated along in that forgettable plane of average.

I chose the Citadel in order to light a fire and burn away my husk of nothingness; to become a man; to set my own gauges of commitment and courage; and to establish the sovereignty of self. Ironically, I found that to do that, I had to erase all boundaries of me and work as part of a larger whole. As you enter the bleak dark forests of its plebe year, you discover with disturbing alacrity that the Citadel journey is not one that can be made alone.

I reported for my freshman year in the fall of 1981. I had just completed my third year as a counselor at the Citadel Summer Camp for Boys and had only left Charleston three weeks before. Now I was returning for an entirely different experience.

Mama drove me down from Rock Hill with my footlocker packed. I had to audition for Regimental Band, but conventional wisdom said if you had even been near a musical instrument in your life, you got put in Band Company. I auditioned and was made bass drummer. Mama and I ate together in the mess hall. After lunch, we said goodbye. It was the second time in my life I ever saw her cry.

I cried too.

I took solace in the fact that I was in familiar territory, having been on the Citadel campus for camp each summer since I was twelve. I felt it to be an intimate and friendly place. Then I met my first sergeant and found out how terribly wrong I was. That first night, I unpacked my belongings. Then at midnight, the cadre forced us to change rooms, repacking and unpacking again. As I settled in with my second roommate the door burst open at nearly 2 in the morning and the upperclassmen forced us to move yet again. Thus the tone was set.

For most of my teenage years, I went to church regularly. That is to say twice a year: Christmas and Easter. My orthodoxy changed quite significantly the day I entered my freshman year at the Citadel.

August 19, 1981 was a Wednesday. It was also Hell Night for 650 matriculating freshman cadet recruits at The Military College of South Carolina. Night had fallen, but we were summoned en masse to assemble on the quadrangle of our barracks.

We stood at rigid attention as "Home Sweet Home" rang out tinny and sweet over the PA system. Squeaky iron gates clanged shut, ending our days as civilians—our years as happy, carefree boys—with an inarguable, defeated, and metallic finality. The disembodied voice of our regimental commander intoned over the PA with all the seriousness of an undertaker: "Gentleman of the Class of 1985, the fourth class system is now in effect."

Then out of the shadows marched phalanx after phalanx of screaming cadre men with hot breath and the fierceness of banshee warriors. They vowed to run us all out. They vowed to exercise us until we vomited or passed out. The devil holds a special place for frightened, nervous, fat mama's boys who test their metal in the crucible of the Citadel.

"You're never gonna make it!" The voice came from behind me. It was the drum major, a senior with whom I'd spent the last six weeks as a counselor at camp. Then we had been friends. Then we had been equals. That night, everything changed.

After Hell Night, I joined the Baptist Student Union, though in all honesty, I would have donned a yarmulke or built a shrine to Buddha if I thought it would have helped me escape the wrath of the cadre. I remember many a Wednesday night after evening mess, sitting around with a group of young men and a guitar-playing youth minister in blue jeans singing "Amazing Grace." I look back on those times and think the only thing separating us from some beatnik band of Jesus freaks on any other college campus in the fall of 1981 was our shaved heads and gray uniforms. We all believed fervently in salvation. We all needed to believe in it because that was what we were desperately seeking.

From Hell Night through Recognition Day, fear, uncertainty, insecurity, and terror governed our every thought, our every action. By the end of the first week, a third of our freshmen class had quit. By year's end, our original numbers were down by half. They sound harsh, these descriptions of yelling young men, but the Citadel stands by its belief that in order to be rebranded as one of its graduates, one must first be rent asunder. In a world of rough seas and hurricane winds, it takes a mighty captain to right and steer the ship. While my high school classmates at USC, Winthrop, or Clemson were going to frat parties and sorority mixers, I was attending parades, scrubbing the barracks' floors, and standing at attention for a Saturday morning inspection. Ours was a Spartan existence. For those of us who gutted it out, the Citadel's greatest blessing is that we are friends, blood brothers, soul mates all.

The Citadel can be a place of seeming incongruity. The most beautiful place on campus is Summerall Chapel, a safe harbor for weary spirits and a place to give thanks for blessings.

Its pastors claim that this masterpiece of stone, stained glass, and pine wood is nonsectarian, belonging to no religion, which makes it at the same time belong to every religion. It is built in the shape of a cross, with clay-red roof tiles contrasting with the white stone exterior. When its thick wooden doors close behind you and your eyes adjust to the light, you are transformed. The flags of fifty states hang from the walls and the light dances with purples, greens, and blues from sun filtering through the windows. It looks perfectly medieval, with its floor of wide flagstones that seem freshly hewn from a mountainside. Iron chandeliers hang from a ceiling of exposed beams and light the path to the altar flanked by choir lofts. I went there often to pray.

My sophomore year I had particular reason to visit the chapel and give thanks. Some friends and I were driving to the Citadel beach house on the Isle of Palms for a party. We shifted lanes and accidently cut off a car filled with other college-aged boys. They honked the horn, cursed us, and shook their fists. We weren't looking for a fight, so we let them pass. It wasn't a good-enough gesture. They pulled in front of us, slammed on brakes, and forced us from the road. My classmate, Jimmy Bowen, was driving our car and he gunned it, driving around them in the grass. They hit the gas and

Summerall Chapel.
Drawing by Mike Strantz, courtesy of Heidi Strantz Mortimer.

followed. Jimmy drove into the beach house parking lot slinging gravel and dust. The boys followed us and jumped out with a tire iron, clenched fists, and obscenities.

Now, there is a fair amount of rivalry between the companies at the Citadel, and band guys took a lot of flack. We carried musical instruments, not rifles. Because we had all been musicians rather than athletes in high school, we tended to place toward the bottom in intramural sports. At that beach house, I didn't expect what happened next.

Somebody saw the commotion and went around to the beachside of the house to raise the alarm. I'm certain less than ten seconds had gone by. I was tensing my body, raising my forearms up to my face getting prepared to get punched.

First I heard them. Then I saw them—three hundred cadets from every class, every battalion, and every company pouring around each side of the beach house like a rainstorm in full fury. Fellow cadets were in danger and they weren't going to have it. I've never seen such a beautiful sight or heard such a wonderful roar. I've also never seen eyes so wide and full of fear as those of the boys who ran back to their car and barely escaped the wrath of the South Carolina Corps of Cadets.

It was at that particular moment, that one second in time that I realized I was as much a part of the Citadel as she was a part of me. When I returned to campus, I went straight to its heart, Summerall Chapel, and gave thanks with a bowed head.

The chapel has etched itself into my character, so much so that often I dream I have returned to the Citadel. Just opposite Summerall Chapel, across the parade ground, sits the iconic 2nd battalion tower of Padgett Thomas barracks, where I lived as a cadet. When you step outside onto Summerall's stone steps, the tower, flying a huge American flag, overtakes your view. This is where my dream begins every time I have it, because each time I left the chapel's magnificent refuge, I emerged prepared, confident, and recharged—ready to take on the seas of troubles life sent my way. It's

merely a dream, some would say. I'm quite convinced, though, that it's the Citadel's way of reassuring me, of saying, "You're one of mine, and you can conquer your challenge."

By entering the Citadel, you swear off everything that's status quo at a "normal college." It is a sacred place sanctified by sweat and tears and history. Ghosts of thousands of my footsteps litter the parade ground in front of the chapel. More times than I can remember, I've done pushups, squat thrusts, and have run, forever running, on that piece of lawn. I have watered its blades of grass with my own sweat and tears. And I have stood at attention watching history as a member of the band that played dirges at the burial of one of World War II's greatest generals,

Cadet Sam Morton.
Photograph courtesy of the author.

Lt. General Mark W. Clark, Allied Commander in Italy and later, president of the college.

The Citadel—in its barracks, on its parade field, and in its classrooms—taught me the great philosophies of life. Some consider the military college that sits on thirteen acres on the Ashley River in Charleston to be the greatest institution of higher education on earth. In truth, the vast majority of those who believe that are her graduates.

Stalwart universities—Harvard, Princeton, Yale—most certainly offer status. The Citadel offers character. And it offers a world rarely seen any more, an atmosphere of *noblesse oblige* in which one's honor is the "immediate jewel" of one's soul.

I go there now and listen to the echoes of my past, the cadence called by our commanders, the cannon as they fired at Friday afternoon parades. I drink in the smell of the freshly mown grass on the parade ground crisp with the scent of wild onion. I even breathe in the musky scent of the pluff mud off the marsh and smile. It is here, in this place, that God answered Jim Heritage's Prayer of the Citadel: God gave the Citadel a boy, and he returned to the world a Citadel man. ☽

Cecile S. Holmes

The Beach House

I long to tell you about fiery, fierce sunsets so yellow-orange-pink that they seem to defy the color spectrum. And about shimmery silver moons that I could almost swear actually floated atop gently lapping ocean waves sparkling with phosphorous. And the tall lowcountry tales I listened to in my girlhood when a neighbor downed one too many of my daddy's unbelievably strong and tasty Old Fashioneds. See, the story that needs telling began for me along a sliver of the South Carolina coast. It features a few typical elements: lazy days made longer by Daylight Savings Time, icy cold Pabst "Blue Your Mind" beer and slow dancing in flip-flops during a short summer romance. But the story stars a house, nothing more, nothing less, simply a house. Well, actually two houses, but I'll explain that later on.

For thirty-eight years, a beach house and a barrier island represented family, home, stability, and familiarity for me. And even though I never lived there, one lot-and-a-half at the Isle of Palms will always seem more like home than the Columbia house where I grew up. More like home than any house I've owned or lived in since, and I've owned several and lived in more than that during my years of cross-country moves around the Southeast and Southwest as a journalist.

I was fifteen, barely a licensed driver (from dawn to sunset under South Carolina law) when I rode down to the Isle of Palms one weekday with my father. I was working for the summer in the accounts payable department of his office supply company, so getting off in the middle of the week was no problem.

Dad wanted me to "look at" a beach house. He didn't tell me he was thinking of buying the house, or even that such an extravagance was a possibility for our family. Frugal to a fault and always worried the family business he'd taken over after returning from World War II would go under, my father never wasted money. Summers we sweated bullets until he finally bought window air conditioning units for our aging, two-story 1920s-era home. Winters he kept the thermostat so low I wore gloves to write term papers. He never bought himself a new suit until I was well into college. He rarely dined out until I graduated from the University of South Carolina and left to take up newspapering in "the other Carolina."

So the concept of purchasing a BEACH HOUSE, to me a symbol of the rich and the sort of thing only doctors or lawyers could afford, was astounding.

That sultry summer Tuesday, Daddy and I took off in the unusually long, forest-green Buick Electra 225 he drove for seventeen years. Nobody but Daddy drove that car. In retrospect and now acutely aware of my father's deep generosity to the people he loved and the downtrodden folks who wandered into his path, I guess I shouldn't have been surprised at his largesse the day we stole away to look at the BEACH HOUSE.

Soon after we hit the then almost new asphalt of Interstate 26 from Columbia to Charleston, he turned to me and said, "Angel, have you ever driven on the interstate before?"

"No, sir," I answered.

"Well, it's time you learned," he replied.

And learn I did. After spending at least five minutes adjusting the seat so my short legs could reach the accelerator and brake, we took off. My father didn't cotton to speeding. "Jack up my insurance rates," he explained as I drove. "Not worth it." We didn't sing hymns, college fight songs or 1940s ditties as we usually did on a road trip. I was too nervous, and my father too intent on teaching me well. Keep a steady speed, he instructed; "We'll get better gas mileage. Make certain you're at least three car lengths behind the fellow in front of you. Now don't you worry, we're going to pass that big truck. I'll tell you how."

By the time we got to the old—the really, really old—Cooper River Bridge, I was passing trucks with aplomb. Or so my father assured me.

But back to the BEACH HOUSE.

When we strolled into the two-story, yellow-and-brown, beach-front house on the Isle of Palms, I almost immediately started party planning. The house included two completely separate apartments, with two kitchens and two screened porches—and perfect in my mind for summer teenage soirees where parents stayed upstairs. Designed to house an intergenerational family of grandparents, parents and children, the house had been built in 1952. For years, it was something of a landmark, the last house on the Isle of Palms—and then nearly the last house—before Palm Boulevard veered to the left leading to the Citadel Beach House and eventually to undeveloped land that included sprawling old trees and a lagoon. My younger brother and I were forbidden to explore that part of the island, but we snuck down there anyway. It reminded us of the book *Robinson Crusoe* and the Disney movie *The Swiss Family Robinson.*

We had to rent out that first house for many years to be able to keep it, a reality my father abhorred, especially when he'd return to discover broken lamps, furniture in the living room that belonged in the bedroom and fishing tackle in drawers assigned to flatware. Many friends and family stayed there for a week, a weekend or simply overnight. Four decades later, my college roommate remembered it as "the quintessential South Carolina beach house." A junior high chum remarked, "Now that, that was a beach house." The memories it engendered always led me and mine to that "sand in my shoes" and "not a care in the world" feeling.

The house hosted multiple house parties for my mother's bridge club, an organization that survived for fifty-odd years and included some of the world's funniest and most adept card-playing steel magnolias. Photographs and home movies of the "girls only" house parties featured the latest swimsuit fashions, clusters of polka-dotted and flower-trimmed sunhats, new makeup techniques, ample supplies of alcohol and endless casseroles. The occasional house parties including "the husbands" were almost as interesting. Sometimes the guys grilled, but they rarely bothered to talk business and only occasionally went fishing. They were simply having too much fun being together.

Over the years the Isle of Palms changed, going from a slow-moving coastal town of a few permanent residents and loads of summer tourists to a more resort-like place with front-beach condominiums, the posh Wild Dunes development and summer tourists from the Eastern Seaboard and beyond. But my feelings about the island never changed. I moved from Greensboro, North Carolina to Houston, Texas, and learned to love the Lone Star State's Gulf Coast. Still, I always returned to the Isle of Palms, lured by its beauty and the proximity of Charleston just fifteen minutes away.

Then came Hurricane Hugo, which made landfall on the island September 21–22, 1989. More than two decades after it struck, I still remember the devastation I saw when I returned seven months later to write a travel story for the *Houston Chronicle.* "God's country," as I jokingly called it, had been hit and hit hard. Charleston was fighting to bounce back. Recovery moved more slowly on my beloved island.

On the island's back streets, I noticed how much debris remained, how many tall, slender palms and their smaller cousins, palmettos, were still bent almost double. Nearby were towering stacks of planks, tree limbs, insulation, shingles and other assorted building materials. In wood alone, Hugo's 135-mile-per-hour winds cost South Carolina dearly. An early estimate set the cost of destroyed saw timber and pulpwood at $1.04 billion. One state forestry official said thirty-six percent of the state's 12.2 million acres of forests were punished by Hugo's tumultuous winds.

When it hit, my mother lay dying in Columbia. Beside her, my father tried desperately to figure out what was going on 110 miles away. He had a phone, but no electricity and therefore no television for more than a week. What he could learn about the storm he heard on the radio and through long-distance phone conversations with my brother in Los Angeles and me in Houston. We watched the storm's path on television with that all-too-familiar certainty long-time coastal residents know so well. Our luck had run out. This time our island and the BEACH HOUSE took an almost direct hit. Actually it was the storm surge, we realized later, that destroyed the house.

We conjectured that the house's bottom half, made of concrete block sturdy enough to survive multiple licks of hurricane-force winds through the years, simply imploded and washed away in the surge. The top half floated, drifted, or something, to bump into a house on the street behind us. When my father and first cousin were allowed on the island several weeks later, my father climbed into what was left of the house's top half to find stainless steel flatware in the silverware drawer and whiskey safely upright in the liquor cabinet.

Eventually my father—then a determined septuagenarian—built another more elaborate and beautiful house. My nieces know that house as "Papa's BEACH HOUSE." One of my godsons dubbed the sparkling surf out front "Aunt Cecile's Ocean."

But Hugo's toll on my father, my family, and me was horrendous. Fate is often cruel in its timing. My mother loved the first BEACH HOUSE, going there every chance she had and sharing it easily. At the beach, she didn't worry much about her hair or makeup, or even a lot about her weight (always an issue). It was she, a peaches-and-cream redhead who had to stay out of the sun, who taught me to love swimming in the moonlight while Daddy stood guard with a flashlight on the beach. It was her dogs, frisky Scottish terriers, which took to crab hunting at night following the flashlight we shone in front of them. She kept the records required of resort property owners who rented out such houses. She listened to my father curse and moan when renters treated the house like a low-rent motel. And it was she who was beside my father when Hugo destroyed the house. Months after her death in February 1990, my father told me he would have had to sell the house if Hugo hadn't destroyed it. "That was Anne's house," he insisted.

Building the second house, my father opted for a five-bedroom, five-bath place with a Jacuzzi tub and a bidet. The latter was installed because it reminded Daddy of a villa where he'd lived in Florence during World War II as part of the American forces that liberated Italy. Over my next twenty years of life—which included an unhappy divorce and a joyful remarriage—that second house became as important to me as the first, but for different reasons. It was where I came to see my brother and his family on vacation from California. It was where I hosted close friends on the East Coast after I married a man who loved Texas and the Gulf Coast even more than I. When I returned to Columbia and became an associate professor in the University of South Carolina's School of Journalism and Mass Communications, it was where my husband Jace and I spent several New Year's Eves, one Christmas and an important birthday. It was where I reconnected with cousins I had lost touch with during the twenty-three years I lived away from South Carolina.

And it was where I came on vacation three years after my mother's death only to have my father tell me there was "someone he wanted me to meet." That someone became my stepmother, whom I learned to love and appreciate. Her daughter and granddaughter grew to love the second house as much as I had loved the first.

When he moved into his eighties, my indomitable father's health began to fail. Eventually he completely lost his ability to walk and suffered from bouts of dementia. But he never forgot the BEACH HOUSE. Nor did I. We used to talk about it after he was sick and miserably imprisoned in a bed and wheelchair. One semester I spent two days a week helping care for him. Sometimes I just stood guard making sure he didn't try to get out of bed, forgetting he could no longer walk. Other times we watched old movies. And one day I'll never forget, I edited copy from my USC senior writing classes while Daddy watched the TV Guide channel for two hours. It was so hard to see someone with such a fine mind decline so quickly. But it was even more important that I was able to be with him. That was the only way I really had to love him when he got so sick.

Some months before my father's death, it was decided that the BEACH HOUSE had to be sold. Our family was crushed. Jace and I agreed to clean

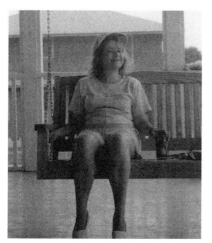

The author and her father, James G. Holmes, on the porch of the second beach house, 1990s. Photograph courtesy of Cecile S. Holmes.

The second Holmes family beach house, about 2000.
Photograph courtesy of Cecile S. Holmes.

out nineteen-some years of belongings. I spent weekends unloading closets, dressers, kitchen cabinets. My brother and his children were crestfallen. So was their first cousin, my oldest niece. Not only was their beloved grand-father dying, their South Carolina touchstone would be gone.

I could tell you what literally happened to the second house and to that lot-and-a-half. But what matters most to me is what happened after the house was sold. Much of it was sad, another cruel convergence of fate. And some of it, just a little, turned out happy with the sort of promise hopeful people see in sunrises, a baby's first steps and college graduations. Less than two years after the house was sold, my father died after months of decline—his beloved wife beside him. This time it was my stepmother who cared for him.

A short thirty-three days after my father died, my husband—recovering from foot surgery—died in his sleep from a heart attack. The coroner told me it was undetected cardiovascular disease. All I knew was that I awakened one Monday morning to find him dead beside me. Losing him—he was only fifty-one—was worse in so many ways than losing my father. It was months before I felt capable of mourning my father. I wandered around, functioning, teaching, writing, sort of in a preoccupied state of shock and grief. I either didn't sleep at all or I slept twelve hours at a time. I didn't know what to do with myself and I missed the ocean and the BEACH HOUSE with my whole heart.

Always and forever, that first house and in many ways the second one will represent home, family, peace, and happiness for me. I believe, and I really don't care if people think I'm "getting a little batty," that my mother's spirit lives at the Isle of Palms. And there has been at least one time when I felt my father had joined her.

I won't drive past the property where the two houses stood. The idea of going within blocks of it paralyzes me. And I did not want to go back to the Isle of Palms.

Then my brother came to visit from Los Angeles and he and my step-mother started talking about getting our extended family together. Eventu-ally they went down towards Charleston to look at houses we might rent for a week. I kept asking, "Can't we go to Folly Beach? Or Pawleys Island? Or Sullivan's Island?" But none of the houses they considered, except on the Isle of Palms, had what they wanted. My brother called me and said, "Okay, the house we want to rent is on the Isle of Palms. But it is at the other end of the island from where our house was. Will you come? It won't be a family vacation without you."

I abhorred the idea. But my nieces and step-niece, my brother, my sister-in-law, my stepsister and my stepmother—now my family—were too much of a drawing card. I drove down in July 2010, talking to the dog and to my deceased husband most of the way. "I don't know if I can do this. I want to. I really want to, but it is so hard."

As I drove, I replayed the last day Jace and I were at the second house. He suggested I try a symbolic ritual before we drove away. We were married on the Texas Gulf Coast under sun-dappled skies amidst aromas of barbecued chicken and slow-smoked beef brisket. We had planned a trip to Texas for a wedding anniversary, and though we made it, we never managed to renew our vows at the old-timey hotel where we'd honeymooned. We thought we had plenty of time to do it later.

For lots of reasons that time never came. So at Jace's suggestion, I took the new vows we had written, wrapped them in a plastic bag and tucked them in a small corked bottle. Going against my environmental conscience, I walked down to the ocean while Jace waited in the car. I tossed in the bottle, took one last look at the house and raced back to my husband.

Too much loss. Too much change in too short a time, my heart told me. But life sometimes is about loss, sorrow, and cruel fate. It also is about hope, recovery, and new beginnings. My week at the beach in a rented house with my family turned out better than I expected.

My nieces—mostly babies, toddlers and 'tweens when they came to the other house—are now young women. They come equipped with tons of makeup and shampoo and can run through bath towels faster than I can wash them. But one of them is turning into a gourmet cook. The oldest, now in her twenties, is wise beyond her years and a loving, quiet anchor in my now-solo life. Another hopes to be a scientist or veterinarian. The youngest is sixteen, with a gentle manner and loving spirit.

Like generations of parents (and aunts and uncles), they are my hope. They make me laugh. They trust me enough to tell me things they won't tell their parents. They love my dog. They think I'm funny. They clap when my brother and I sing classic rock n' roll together. They think I'm smart, asking me questions about my favorite subjects, pop culture and religion, and listening to my answers. And they are there when I need to talk about what I've lost.

I tell them stories about their grandfather and their uncle, and they listen. What more could I ask? ☽

Photo courtesy of Dr. Benjamin E. Mays Historical
Preservation Site, Greenwood, South Carolina.

The Ever-Present Past

"I am disturbed, I am uneasy about men because we have no guarantee that when we train a man's mind, we will train his heart; no guarantee that when we increase a man's knowledge, we will increase his goodness. There is no necessary correlation between knowledge and goodness."

Educator, minister, and Epworth native Benjamin E. Mays (1894–1984), president of Morehouse College and a mentor to Martin Luther King, Jr.

Nick Lindsay

☾

The Fiery Serpent in the Wilderness

Before the Anti-Preaching Edict

Out of breath, who can help it? Climb up, climb up, away from the dump trucks, bulldozers, 300-horsepower Ingersol-Rand air compressors. Poof! Here on high whipped by this western Bum Plant wind, oh Jesus! Drop one nail and you can count to five before it hits. If I fall off? Whee-splat! A cornpone in a casserole. Feel easy? No way. What are we doing *here*? We're topping out this 105-C, the last of the five great reactors of this three-hundred-square-mile Bum Plant.

Fall off here? Squash like a bug, goodbye. What have we climbed up here for? It's to bolt these ton-and-a-half twenty-by-twenty-foot concrete form panels solidly to the ones on the other side, yes, and Larry Bent's wild concrete crew's going to dump their five-ton buckets of concrete tomorrow morning.

Our job's to Makum solid? Well, you bet! It's what we're standing on, tied off to. Tied off here on high with a single 5/8-foot safety rope. I tie off with a clove hitch mostly. Each time my toe slips—poof! Heart attack time. It's a long way *down.*

Yes, and when Old Bud's coming around taking names? Kingdom Come. Push me a tie rod through to Mr. Harry, my old partner climbed up on the other side. Jesus Christ have mercy on him and me too.

Screaming! What? It's Reverend Red. What? Right here on *high*?

"Oh the fiery POW*!"*

He's squalling as he drives his steel.

Fear of heights wasn't recommended for Savannah River Site employees.
Photograph courtesy of Savannah River Nuclear Solutions, LLC.

"Fiery Serpent POW! *In the wilderness* POW!
Jesus, Fiery Serpent POW! *Of my soul* POW!
Oh the Wilderness POW! *Oh my own, true Jesus* POW!"

Reverend Red, yeah and yay-hooray for all the Jesus we can get here in our peril on high! And below us all the huge tumult and plunder of construction—bulldozers, dump trucks and dust clouds, compressors, loudspeakers—all.

Fiery red hair, washed-out blue eyes, Red screams out the loveliness of Jesus, the glories of Jesus, the Fiery Serpent in this Wilderness. He commutes every dawn from up near Walhalla in the northwest corner of the state, first came to us at the end of last year. Drunk. Another whiskey wreck of a skinny Scots-Irish mountaineer. He was helped and shepherded through those first days by Old Man Strothers who comes to us from down around Savannah. What a good old man!

But one morning last May, May of 1953, he got Christ-bit (as it's said in the crafts here). He saw the light, sobered up, and started in to preaching in his reedy, passionate screams. If you have heard seagulls' inchoate, glorious screaming as they follow behind trawlers across the trackless, fish-wealthy tides of early summer, you have some idea of Red's sermons.

Only those of us who are tied off perilously here have ever heard him. No security guard nor no head-count man with his clickers is going to climb so high nor risk so much just in his appointed rounds. No, no.

But for us it is possible to forget the hungry abyss, forget the wide invitation to leap out into the caressing, empty air, forget the blisters and torn hide as we grapple our way ever-upward twenty feet at a time with Reverend Red's passionate screams to numb our rational terror and reassure us. Though the Fiery Serpent has struck us with his deadly fangs and man-killing venom, He can still sneak in here that we might cry out in our worship and survive yet another sunset, another daybreak.

In South Carolina, the musty dusty old guard of our Lost Cause aristocracy has always claimed to be governed by Honor. The idea is that the highest status in our society is granted to the person who is seen to strut on the public stage of politics his posture erect even though his daughters Goneril and Regan are gouging out his eyes, fleas are biting all up and down his spine, and he has some imperative physiological urge hammering within his entrails. *Robert E. Lee even unto the death! I could not love thee, dear, so much, loved I not honor more!*

R. G. Bruce, yonder down this very wall, is honorable through and through. We call him "The Bruce." He goes foxhunting with a Ford V8 on full-moon nights, following the hounds, crashing through fences and walls, disregarding ditches and cornfields—ruins the Ford, but brings him to be held in the highest public honor all across the Piedmont. He will tolerate no public insult nor known thwarting of his intentions. His public self will accept nothing less than The Truth in any public exchange. The word "public" is what counts. If the neighbors don't know, the details of his disregard of ethics don't matter at all. The Bruce. "I, sir, am an honorable man, sir (knife pointed to your goozle); admit it or your deal's gone down, sir!"

His partner with the splintered teeth, Benton over there, comes from Charleston, and is in no way hampered by any such "honor" fantasy.

This Bum Plant project is as huge as any undertaking known to man—the Egyptian pyramids, or Babylon the Great; the Suez Canal, or the Atom Bomb Plant in Oak Ridge, Tennessee—any. We're greater by far than Troy, the source of all the Homeric hero tales told by the Greek Orthodox Painters' Union up from Florida. We have made nine different cities in our three-hundred-square-mile area, and each one by itself is bigger than Troy ever was. Our reactor, 105-C alone was bigger than Chernobyl, at which the whole world trembled when it blew. Yet we made *five* of them and blew up nary a one!

If it's so big, how come so many people in South Carolina or the rest of the world don't know anything about it? It's because the U.S. Government and the Atomic Energy Commission have tried to keep it such a super secret all these years.

If we take just one of the nine Bum Plant cities, it makes a better comparison to Homer's Troy. For the whole project, all the other eight cities' materials and administrations come from Central Shops: maybe it'll be the most doable. Okay, Central Shops versus Homeric Troy:

Some Comparative History

Ancient Troy, City Beloved by the Immortal Gods
and by the Florida Greek Painters' Union
Compared to
Present-day Central Shops, Destructive Center of the Universe:
Troy 1250 B.C.: 30° 54' north latitude, 26° 8' east longitude, 175 miles southwest from Constantinople, halfway to Athens, Greece. Start northwest from today's archaeological site, go 6,600 miles, up across Berlin, Ireland, Newfoundland, then down southwest and land at Central Shops, an area five times as large as was the walled city of Troy. Troy was known of old as Ilium, was on the river Scamander. Ilium, Priam, Paris—all these names from Homer's songs stamp them as coming from the Hittite kingdoms— what has become modern Turkey. Troy was that citadel of the far-reaching merchant empire that controlled the Dardanelles and the sea passage between the Mediterranean and Black seas, and where the Homeric exploits of Hector and Achilles and the Olympian gods took place. Just ask anyone from the Sarasota Painters' Union.

Compare: Central Shops of 1960 A.D. is still alive, and located 35° 15' north latitude, 81° 40' west longitude, 150 miles west northwest from Columbia, halfway to Athens, Georgia, and located in Barnwell County on the Savannah River. Dangerfield, Terrapin, Shumpert, Ott, Seay, Bailey, Foley— all these our South Carolina names stamp us as coming from some fantasy or accident of language feeding into the girlish dream of moonlit magnolia leisure and nobility, hideous dream of terror and nausea in the shadow of the Ku Klux Klan, its "Mounted Rifles," and its white hoods.

Early construction site.
Photograph courtesy of Savannah River Nuclear Solutions, LLC.

To the credit of Du Pont and the Atomic Energy Commission, it's worth noticing that more men were fired for being "members of a secret society devoted to the overthrow of the U.S. Government" when they were found to be members of the KKK than when they were identified as members of the Communist Party. We lost a great comedian, Jonesie, from the 100-C tool room for that. He thought it was a joke, but Du Pont didn't.

1200 B.C.: Ramses II rules in Egypt: The Egyptian Empire is about to swallow all the known world. Agamemnon's Achaean warriors, on their way home after finishing off Troy forever, raid Egypt's coasts, steal people, cattle, bronze ornaments, kill, rape, and rob; and Ramses II is so busy fighting off this swarm of stinging, stinking Greeks that he accidentally lets Moses and his little gang of service personnel steal the family silver out of all the upper-caste houses and run off into the desert. After several seasons of monotonous diet and wilderness wandering, the peasant-slaves grumble against Moses and God; God makes a plague of stinging, deadly serpents to terrify the gang but shows Moses how to make a bronze serpent—anyone who worships this idol even briefly will be cured of snakebite. Hooray for the Fiery Serpent in the Wilderness!

But woe unto Ilium, AKA Troy and all her line of Hittite kings! The brutal Greeks have wiped 'em out. Earth knows them no more, and never again will they be found by the all-seeing sun in any of his daily rounds.

Compare: 1945 A.D.: Harry ("Give 'em Hell") Truman rules in the U.S.A. The U.S. empire has just whipped all the known world. Woe unto Hitler's war-weary child soldiers! They must fight on, kill, rape, and rob, though in retreat.

May 8, Mother's Day, 1945, VE Day. Victory in Europe. August 6: We vaporize a significant portion of Hiroshima with an atomic bomb; then ten days later, August 16, 1945, VJ Day: World War II is done. The U.S.A. has the atomic bomb, the only one there ever was. No one can ever challenge us again. If the Soviets become troublesome, wound our honor, or break our hearts, we can vaporize 'em. *Hooray for us!*

But then, Oh then! Stalin gets the A Bomb!
And blows one off just to prove it!
And what will God say about that?

As it turns out, God molded and fashioned with His muddy hands a certain element called hydrogen. He made it back in Genesis, along with all the rest. Not only this, but He caused there to be born men called "the fathers of the H Bomb"—Teller, Bohr, Oppenheimer. One child with three fathers? How sordid! But we need to admit, it's a very big bomb, and can be made as big as any politician's ambition. Needs three fathers at the very least.

The Soviets have Andrei Sakharov. Okay. Four fathers.

But the point is we need a total USA galvanization, and it must be done in utter secrecy if we are to get one ready to blow off before Stalin gets one. It will take a three-hundred-square-mile above-ground installation with forty-five thousand workers on the roads each shift change, which is as many as Agamemnon ever got during the whole ten years of Homer's *Iliad*, and they must come and go at least twice a day, and **not a soul must know a single whisper about any of it!** *In secrecy? You'll say it can't be done, and you're right about that.*

A.D. 1950. Where and what is Williston? It's at 81° 24' west longitude by 33° 24' north latitude, and its known world is a peaceful twenty-mile circle

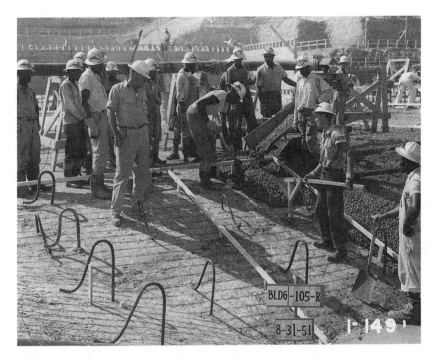

Workers digging at Building 105-R.
Photograph courtesy of Savannah River Solutions, LLC.

of one hundred families, black and white and molasses colored—say about three thousand souls. You can find it on SC Route 39 just north of Barnwell State Park and midway between Elko and White Pond. It has both a post office and a grocery store, Milton's grocery store. He has a gas pump out front, a grease rack out back. If you need salt crackers or sudden cash, fresh milk or first aid, come see Milton. He sells local sweet potatoes, beef raised right here in Barnwell County, and he even has a phone.

Milton says he comes from some Englishman who wrote about going to Hell, "but Williston here is Paradise."

Then it's January of 1951, and The H Bomb Plant comes crashing down onto Williston as on all of us. Williston's population of three thousand increases tenfold in six weeks' time. It becomes a town of thirty thousand Hero-Bums, with our women, wives, and young. We are clouds of strangers like the sudden gnats that swarm in the South Carolina springtime. Gnats penetrate everywhere as do these swarms of us, the unwashed who speak strange dialects, savages who never heard of "The Lost Cause," or

"Confederate Honor" in the way they are spoken of in Edgefield and Barnwell counties by "real" South Carolina folk. We're a rabble of highly skilled men sent from the painters' union in Florida, the sheet metal union in Savannah, the welders' union in New Haven where they weld up submarines for the U.S. Navy, the plumbers' union out in Seattle.

Thirty thousand of us thunder into Williston, camp out in tents in the fields, under overpasses, along the roads, or in the woods. How will we be fed? Friday's payday out at The Project; Milton and our new grocery entrepreneurs arrange for semi-trucks to bring in tons of beef and pork and broccoli every Friday and it's laid out on planks on sawhorses all along these roads. Even schoolteachers can afford to buy it! Lean ground beef is fifty-nine cents a pound, yesterday's Wonderbread is ten cents for a pound-and-a-half loaf, and rent, if you can find a house, is $45 a month! I have a family of eight, including Mama and Papa and the six girls, and we can eat on $23 a week! If this isn't *Hallelujah Amen* ain't nothing going to measure up!

"Oh the Fiery Serpent in the Wilderness, my own, true Jesus!"

The Florida Greeks—the painters' union—know their inherited stories. You just bump into any one of them and he will tell you Homer's *Iliad* on the spot if you ask him, tell it in the original tongue of Peisistratus of 600 B.C.. His Greek Orthodox Bible? He has it by heart in the original Aramaic. You just ask him the least little question and bushels of Saint Paul's letters come spilling out: *"Ean tois glosois ton anthropon lalo, kai ton angelon, agapain de me echo, gegona khalkos echon y kumbalon allalazon . . ."* (Though with the tongues of men I speak, and of angels, but if love I have not, I become an echoing brass and a cymbal with its al-la-la, a-la-la).

Love indeed, or at least charity and mercy, yes, for no matter how many welcoming "blind tigers" spring up along our sandy roads that wind in their despairing secrecy through the woods seeking our worksites, and no matter how many people join unions or talk politics, *no hot lead!* Or almost none. Even for black people.

Jonesie, our tool man in 100-C that got fired for being a dragon or court jester or something for the Birmingham KKK used to say, "And what is it then? Have ye all gone soft, or what?"

Up until now, if you were black and went to register to vote, you didn't wonder whether those men walking around the registration place were armed. No, but your only question was, "How good a shot are they?" Lead poisoning still presented a health problem for those of us in the black community who risked registering to vote, or in the white community choosing to join a union.

In 1950 when we started this Bum Plant, here in this corner of South Carolina it was just sixteen years previously that seven men were killed and a woman shot in the town of Honea Path at their textile mill picnic by the rag-tag Chiquola Manufacturing Company's militia under the leadership of Dan Beacham the town mayor. In the crew I started in back in 1950 when I quit teaching and started eating regularly, there were sixteen carpenters, two colored laborers and one little bitty Muslim welder, my then-partner, Mustafa. Among the whole of us there was not one who didn't frown and shut up if you mentioned Honea Path. No one except Mustafa, and he came from New Haven, Connecticut. Of course all those men felt terrible about it! Kinsman had shot kinsman, uncles and nephews had shot unarmed aunties and little cousins. Who could stand it?

There in Honea Path, the corpses were white for a change. Then, after that the unfortunate picnic came to be called "The Honea Path Massacre," and in keeping with the racial discomforts of the times, we had to find some *white* body bags. Not only this, but since we were good tithing church folk we refused 'em any Christian burial. Come on! What d'you expect of us? Who but Chiquola Manufacturing was paying the church budget and the preacher's salary?

We exiled those corpses from their own home churchyards for just talking union in a tiny whisper—Honea Path, Ware Shoals, up in there. But here now we have forty-five thousand union folk, men and women with their children, tricycles, and puppy dogs, assembled to build an H Bomb and not a one of us shot for it! How about that! All Saint Paul needed was a little bitty old H Bomb and the world would be a peaceful, merciful, and charitable place (as it's set forth in the beginning of Matthew, Temptation #3).

Oh the Fiery Serpent, my own true Jesus tempted in the Wilderness!

According to the Du Pont Corporation in their reports to Congress, it would have been impossible to bring together this forty-five thousand-person army of skilled workers this fast without the unions across the country doing their skillful best to help it happen. At the United Carpenters and Joiners Picnic in the spring of 1952, a sweet day in the city park in Augusta, Georgia, we had more than two thousand of us eating hotdogs and participating in our Soda Pop Paradise, yes! We were men, women, children, and suckling infants who ate those sunshine hotdogs and got home safe and totally unpunctured. Imagine! My own fifth child hadn't yet been weaned. *How good!* Amen.

Saint Paul didn't know about hydrogen, nor, in fact, does the USA Nation either, not until God Almighty causes Niels Bohr to invent his theory of the hydrogen atom in the 1940s and '50s; but Bohr can't finish figuring it out, and how it can be led to release the terrifying energy in its nucleus until months after we have already built this final reactor in our five-reactor spread and left all five of them perking in the photogenic southern sun. Like building a Ford V8 factory before anyone's yet invented a V8 motor! Impossible? Yes, *but we did it! Yes we did! Hooray for us!*

We abolished the countless towns, crossroad villages, and old mossy churches with their graves, their tombs and ancestral hopes. *Now the all-seeing sun will find them never again in any of his daily rounds.*

The Jesus Abolition Edict

We abolished the towns, crossroads, and the churches, but to offset these, new Holy Ghost churches sprang up everywhere, sprang up like wild dandelions speaking with the tongues of men and of angels in trailers, in dead school buses, in the wrecks of houses and blacksmith shops jacked up on wheels as they were dragged off the deadly-national-security-secret property Yes! Even in the bowels of the earth at morning and evening break times and lunchtime in the depths of 105-R, or 105-L, or the windy heights of the 400-D bubble towers—all about! Sacred enthusiasm sang its songs from the public address systems whenever there wasn't a necessary secular communication to put forth. "When the Roll Is Called Up Yonder, I'll Be There," "Send The Fire!" (*Click! Scratchy-scratch*), "Engineer Dale Sennett please call Superintendent Parker at the Three and Seven Hundred Warehouse," or "Area Superintendent Slim Bolin wanted at Planning and Scheduling."

It's the end of April, 1954. Those of us who formed up and poured the reactor base down in the very bottom of 105-C, "The Last of the Five Great Reactors," have grown accustomed to meeting our old preacher there, Boleyn (Jacques C. Boulineau III from zydeco country down in Louisiana). That reactor base is an octagon three feet high, twenty feet across—makes a spacious pulpit platform for any Holy Ghost prophet to tell his story and cry out his pep talk. When the noon whistle screams through our universe, we gather in the broad drain canal on the west side of the reactor base.

But on a certain Wednesday foreordained and predestined and set aside from the beginning of time, the Pipefitter preacher comes hastening out of the eastern Pump Room, rosy daybreak side, Easter's side (as the Highland and Island Scots would identify her); he clambers up on the reactor base. On Tuesdays, Thursdays, and Saturdays, he has been proclaiming the perfections of his Pipefitter Jesus, taking turns with Reverend Boley. Our prophet has Mondays, Wednesdays, and Fridays for our Carpenters' and

Joiners' Jesus. But what are all these pipefitters doing here today, Wednesday? It's Boley's day, and they know it! What is going to happen now?

Rev. Pipefitter: "Remember! Oh ye pipefitters! At the Name, every knee shall bend, every head shall bow! God loves! Our only true sacrifice is a pipe well run, a joint welded with no leak, and all the perfections we can ever know! No more jackleg job nor no more of blind blunders to pave our life's pathways [Second Samuel 5:6]. Remember you are a pipefitter! It is excellence of skill that gives you your name, your badge number, and your place out here in the government parking lot!" (Must be they had a bad mess-up running pipe this morning. It isn't easy when the craft blueprints that come straight from Wilmington don't agree with one another).

And so forth. His amen row of grimy parishioners has hurried in from the eastern Pump Room to support him. Reverend Boley's amen row has already assembled here on the west, that region of darkness, shadows and ancient death (according to Seay and Terrapin and our American Indian carpenters).

But now Boley climbs up! The two prophets eye one another. Who is going to win? They square off, they lower their heads, they move slowly centerward with a sort of measured ecclesiastical pace from east and west on their hexagonal pulpit. The amen rows are squatted attentively.

The merciful Du Pont safety program requires that the reverends keep their tin hats on at all times, even when preaching The Word. The two hats clash. They say *Ding!* Say *clankety-clank!* Now Rev. Pipefitter is weeping wordlessly. He floors Rev. Boley with a mighty blow. The two amen rows say, "*Amen!*"

Reverend Boley is wearing his brand-new twenty-dollar guaranteed-not-to-rip-or-tear Sears Roebuck white duck overalls and they are loaded with sixteen-penny nails, eight-penny double-headed nails, quarter-inch bolts with washers and nuts, claw hammer, try square, rule, crescent wrench, side-cutting pliers, a hand roll of baling wire—the works. If you mean to accomplish anything, you have to carry this hardware all through the day—usually about fifty pounds—climb high, crawl low with all this hanging from your shoulder straps. When Reverend Boley hits the deck his overalls make a mournful crash. He gets to his feet. He means to continue the dialogue. *Martin Luther debating with the Papal emissary at Worms.* A left! A right! Reverend Pipefitter's tin hat has rolled off into the gutter that runs around the perimeter of the chamber. If our Safety Engineer (a Boy Scout leader/schoolteacher named Godsey) were to see him and make a case, his pipefitting days out here would be done.

As it turns out, some spoilsport calls Security and both disciples are led off and summarily fired. Fighting on the job is strictly prohibited here where we've nearly finished making the locus of production of the most deadly weapon the world has ever imagined. But worse than the firing of these prophets is

The Edict

The command comes from Du Pont on high (= Wilmington, Delaware), to Central Shops, from Central Shops to Planning and Scheduling in each area, from Planning and Scheduling to all Area Craft Superintendents, and thence to all superintendents and foremen whatsoever (= Ott Zion): NO MORE JESUS IN ANY SHAPE OR KIND ON THE WHOLE SAVANNAH RIVER SITE!

Woe unto all perilous laborers in this Western Carolina garden of renewed hope and world terror!

But will we give in? *No!* (By next week, we high-climbers in Ott Zion's crew have utterly refused! Our God is the only high-climbing and Fiery Serpent who slips His skin and whips His way on high in all this wilderness! No security man, nor any engineer will ever climb hand-over-hand up 150 feet into the sun-buzz of the sky nor risk his soft skin to prohibit our arduous worship. We will climb up, tie off, and pound out our gladness on high, reassured by the lovely succession of payday groceries, and by our outlaw Jesus and our own wild-eyed Reverend Red. He screams,

"Children of Israel! Oh snake-bit and ruined!
Us here, oh! Hit bit and ruined by money wages, money is dirt!
Find a dollar? Give it away by lunchtime! Dirt and spiritual garbage!
Canned fish and rotten politics!
Oh the terrors of God, the deadly serpents in the wilderness!

Children of Israel! Stink-dying all about!
But Saved, yes, they looking on the Fiery Serpent!
We can be saved! Oh, look our canned money politics straight in
   the eye!
Our souls sold for a dollar and a half, our dirt graves paved over,
Oh my Untame Jesus! My Fiery Serpent in this wilderness!

And now I am old, and ready to be gone, I get to thinking over what I've been and done, my woman's trouble, my children's hardship and pain, but O my Fiery Serpent, I'd do the very same thing again!

In those days so long ago, it was possible to forget the hungry abyss, the wide temptation to leap out into self-obliteration, the yawning, empty air, forget the blisters and torn hide as we grappled our way ever upward twenty feet at a time through the whips of that western wind with Reverend Red's passionate screams to reassure us that in spite of THE EDICT, our Fiery Serpent could still slither, twist and wind His way upward on high with us, and His prophet could scream out His power to bring victory out of impossibility: yes.

We poured and finished 3 million tons of concrete
We dumped and graded fifty million tons of secret Western Carolina dirt
We tied and/or welded 645 thousand tons of re-steel
Besides which, any South Carolina schoolteacher achieved at least two
   and a half times his schoolteaching salary by becoming a union crafts-
   man for Du Pont and the Atomic Energy Commission to build their
   Bum Plant (take *that* O thou laborer in the vineyards of literacy!)

During the Civil War, we soldiers of the Lord—U.S. Nation or Confederate Nation—killed out six hundred thousand, counting the men, the women, and the little children, Yankees and southern, black and white, but not counting the cats, dogs, and horses. Death is an equal-opportunity employer.

Yea but, for the building of the Bum Plant, we brought in forty-five thousand *living* people, men, and women, black, white, and molasses-colored. That's as many as Agamemnon brought to wipe out Troy, though just seven and a half percent as many as we killed off in our War of National Certification, and the Bum Plant didn't kill but two on the job in all this time, 1950 to 1955; one an old plumber from Seattle who had a heart attack sitting in one of the latrines in the 105-C reactor building; the other a carpenter in 400-D, who got so mad with his foreman that he snatched up a piece of plywood flooring high in the pump building, stormed off into space and skewered himself on the bristle of re-bars sticking up from below. Ow, ow, ow! *O weep for this prince among the punctured, for he is dead.*

But that leaves 44,998 who walked away rejoicing! A living wage for the first time since the poor people fought the rich men's Civil War.

No slouch of a Bum Plant! ♪

Ceille Baird Welch

A Snapshot of My Mother
at the Dock Street

When my mother dressed she wore a hat and gloves and entered rooms twirling, like Loretta Young. From the first of September and on until spring, when my mother dressed she wore a stole of little foxes draped about her shoulders, each fox bitten to the other, head to tail, the last one hanging free. "There are times a southern woman must pretend to be chilly," she told me, "in order to justify her costume."

There were two well-known certainties about my mother: she was a fearless taker of chance, and she never missed a chance for affectation. Sometimes for expediency she'd unfasten the foxes, would toss them to one side in a carefree way.

I took a snapshot of her with a Kodak Brownie in the early fall of 1954 when I was thirteen. She's in front of the Dock Street Theatre in Charleston's old French Quarter. With one hand curled around the post of a street lamp, the other hand securing her hat, she's sweeping out, her head thrown back, her mouth laughing. The foxes are swinging from her shoulder like a hunting trophy.

"The fellow in yonder at the box office thinks I ought to be onstage," she has just said. "I told him, 'The world is my stage.'" Behind her the Dock Street Theatre's balconies of wrought iron lace are silhouetted against the towering spire of St. Philip's Church.

When I was thirteen, my mother was my best friend. On our special trips to Charleston from Moncks Corner thirty-something miles away, she and I became accustomed to doing certain things. Always pinching our pennies, we'd browse about the shops on King Street, then buy a quarter-pound of chocolate-covered peanuts that we shared.

In pleasant weather we'd stroll along the Battery, or we'd stroll through the Market Place, or we'd stroll along Church Street, past the Dock Street Theatre.

I remember my mother tapping her long red nails against a poster. "Look! Look at this! The Footlight Players are performing *Hansel and Gretel*! An opera for children! And, my darling, contrary to your belief, you're still a child!"

I remember her dark eyes dancing, her eyebrows penciled into high thin arches. "The Footlight Players are the finest in the south. I'll have to see what I can do."

And I remember waiting, making myself dizzy walking round and round the streetlamps, round and round the theater's massive brownstone columns.

Within a recessed porch of stone were three heavy double doors, each with rows of little beveled windows. I could, at first, see only my colorless self repeated in the squares of glass: dirty-blonde-just-turned-teenager with the awkward mouth and the nose. But when I pressed my face hard against a pane, I could see into the dimness of a wine-red lobby, ghostly and regal, with lofty ceilings and a grand double winding stair.

I could make out the tall, slim form of my raven-haired mother, could hear her laughter, as bold as any man's. I saw the foxes when they hopped over her shoulder. I saw her open her handbag.

She finally twirled herself back into the daylight. "Adult tickets are exorbitant," she said, "and that fellow in yonder is determined to consider age thirteen an adult."

Then a smile teased across her bright mouth, curving the edges up, showing off the dramatic little space between her top front teeth. "So . . . I bought your 'adult' ticket with your new-dress money! Oh, don't pout. I'll sew your dress. You know I'm a wonderful seamstress. Now snap a picture of me so that years from now we can look back and remember."

As we hurried away to buy remnants of cloth and sewing notions, my mother looked at me quizzically and said, "You know what that fellow told me? He told me a good southerner courts history like a lover."

At 135 Church Street, on the corner of Church and Queen, the Dock Street Theatre dates to 1736 when Queen Street was Dock Street and need was felt for a building designed expressly for performance. The "new theatre in Dock Street," as it was called by the *South Carolina Gazette,* opened with a comedy, *The Recruiting Officer,* and touted the appearance of a lead

Marian Covington Baird Cochran, about 1945. Photograph courtesy of the author.

actress mysteriously calling herself by the name of another play's tragic heroine, "Monomia."

Only four years later, a great fire destroyed most of Charleston's French Quarter and during the next four decades anything remaining of the original theater was replaced or remodeled several times. There is little documentation on those lost years.

In 1809 Alexander Calder of Charleston renovated several existing structures at the site and added other construction to create a large townhouse. There, Mrs. Calder, his wife, operated not a theater but the upscale Planter's Hotel where wealthy planters converged during horse racing season and where occasional traveling actors stayed.

The banded brownstone columns and the now-famous balconies of deep teal wrought iron filigree were not added until mid-century. It is said that a notable actor of the day, Junius Brutus Booth, father of John Wilkes Booth, sat many an evening on one of those balconies, sipping the establishment's famous punch before the Planter's Hotel fell into deeper and deeper ruin after the Civil War.

The great earthquake of 1886 seemed to seal the old building's fate and by the beginning of the twentieth century, what was once a meeting place for the affluent had become a sadly run-down tenement house—and was soon deemed unfit for even that.

In the 1920s and '30s Charleston's citizenry rallied. They would save the historic building, would call it the Dock Street Theatre again and design it as a theatrical venue. Choosing as their model a composite of eighteenth century London theaters, they put to use salvaged architecture from antebellum churches and mansions, and showcased exquisite new woodwork carved from native cypress trees.

In 1937 it reopened with a commemorative performance of *The Recruiting Officer.* At that opening, Dubose Heyward, known for his novel *Porgy* and his collaboration with Ira Gershwin on the folk opera *Porgy and Bess,* was named writer in residence. April 2010 marked the completion of yet another major renovation.

"You can measure the course of the Dock Street Theatre's history," Charlestonians say, "by counting its myriad colors of brick as one might count rings in a tree trunk."

Ceille Baird Welch outside the Dock Street Theatre. Photograph by Jim Welch.

So here I am, measuring a course of history, inching my fingers around a brownstone column, reflecting resolutely in a square of beveled glass, entering into a stately lobby, and ascending a winding stair.

There are ghosts in this old place. A mysterious actress known only as Monomia is here. And Mrs. Alexander Calder. And Junius Booth. Playwrights Dubose and Dorothy Heyward are here. My mother and I are here too. We're sitting side by side in nineteenth-century church pew seats and because of my mother's hat, we're sitting in the very back row.

It's 1954 and I'm a young girl again. I'm wearing a shirtwaist of brown linen with thirty-six pearl buttons down the front and my mother is leaning toward me. She's reminding me there are also thirty-six buttonholes, which she sewed by hand and that she never intends to let me forget.

As music swells around us, the curtain opens upon a fairy tale setting and characters in brilliant costume saying and singing beautiful words in ways I've never heard.

I'm in love!

I want to speak words like that! I want to feel their rhythms against my tongue! I want to write words like that on paper so that others might speak them and I might hear! I want to set words to melodies.

I want to memorize everything around me as though it were a play script. I want to breathe it all into my lungs so that I might carry it away to wonder about at my leisure, because at this moment I want only to look down upon the Dock Street Theatre's hallowed stage and believe that the world is magical.

In 1963 the old snapshot of my mother at the Dock Street was lost to vandals, but it's not a material snapshot that I'm holding. Neither is it brick and mortar nor musk nor patina nor any singular unmoving thing that holds me now. Rather, it's all those things come together, fluid and sweeping, to carry me along, like time.

It's *Hansel and Gretel* alive in my memory; the Footlight Players as they once were. It's my mother's gloved fingers reaching across the arm of a church pew to intertwine with my own. It's the sly knowing arch of her pencil-thin brow, the secret curving of her bright mouth. It's thirty-six buttonholes down the front of a brown linen dress. And it's the carefree way my mother is always flinging to the side her stole of little foxes. ⟁

W. Thomas Smith Jr.

☽

Pilgrimage to Sullivan's Island

As I write this—234 years after what has been described as the "first decisive victory of American forces over the British Navy" during the American Revolution—I am reminded of one of my many pilgrimages to one of the harbor islands defending the Holy City (Charleston, South Carolina) several years ago.

I say "Holy City" because the affectionate moniker—long known to South Carolinians and only recently as a regular sobriquet in national media—reflects the city's prominence of churches on the low-rise cityscape, the numerous steeples piercing the city's skyline, and the fact that Charleston was one of the few cities in the original thirteen colonies known for its religious tolerance, albeit initially restricted to Catholics, Protestants, and Jews.

For me Charleston is also "the Holy City"—and one to which I make frequent "pilgrimages"—because of its rich southern culture, which has been so naturally interwoven with southern—and a broader American—military history and tradition.

This may sound odd to non-southerners, but there is something to be said for this somewhat uniquely southern military tradition, the fact that there may be something inherent in most southern boys that predisposes them to the profession of arms, and why southern boys (and men) like me grow up to see cities like Charleston as sacred.

"Some historians claim that due to geography, frontier conditions, incessant warfare, slavery, and cultural notions of honor, the south developed into a remarkably militaristic society, fond of military display, preoccupied with war and notions of martial glory, and holding up military service and military training as honorable activities for males," writes Rod Andrew, Jr., in his book *Long Gray Lines.*

And in his book *The Lords of Discipline*—based largely on the Citadel, the storied Charleston-based Military College of South Carolina—author Pat Conroy writes, "No southern man is complete without a tenure under military rule."

I know for a fact I would not be complete without my own tenure in Uncle Sam's Marine Corps, which is itself an institution heavily influenced by all things southern (even South Carolinian).

So Charleston for me is sacred ground—land and sea—and at no time did I ever feel a more spiritual connection to the city than in October 2003, when I made a pilgrimage there. I was teaching a class sponsored by the now-defunct Southern Literature Council of Charleston. The class—actually more of a workshop composed of College of Charleston professors, aspiring novelists, and a few struggling poets—was great. But the highlight of the trip was where I spent the night: a gloriously quiet beachfront manse built in 1869 (just a few years after the close of the Civil War in 1865) on Charleston's Sullivan's Island, the aforementioned harbor island defending Charleston.

The house was located on Middle Street, a dead-end road on Sullivan's just a few hundred yards from Fort Moultrie (yes, the former Fort Sullivan where South Carolina earned its own sobriquet as The Palmetto State). I actually clocked the distance in my car, and it was less than one-tenth of a mile from the house to Moultrie's huge concrete-and-brick walls.

This was not the first time I'd visited Charleston or Sullivan's Island. I had traveled here many times as a small boy and teenager. And I was stationed at the Naval Weapons Station on North Charleston's stretch of the Cooper River for two of my four years in the Marine Corps, during which I made many trips to Fort Moultrie. Here I strolled the corridors and ramparts of the old bastion—which had undergone multiple upfits over the years, walked on the beach between the fort and the sea, ran in the surf, swam beyond the breakers, brought girls, and enjoyed the quietude away from my wild, testosterone-jacked buddies.

But it was always the fort, more than the beach, the babes, and the breakers, that restored my soul. The fort was always the spiritual draw.

Damaged by war, decayed by salt air, the sea, years of neglect, and more than one hurricane, upfitted and rebuilt, Moultrie's history spans that of America's own timeline. Today, visitors will find the fort constructed of thick concrete and steel. Much of the work was completed soon after the conclusion of the Civil War, with its most recent batteries and emplacements now a testament to its final service as a World War II Harbor Entrance Control

Fort Sumter.
Photograph by Patrick Wright.

Post on watch for enemy submarines. But the spirit of the old palmetto-log fort remains.

Sullivan's has since become a very familiar place to me. But an afternoon, a night, and a morning alone—with the exception of a few ghosts—in the house on Middle Street was a special, unique experience. The house, owned by the family of Ms. Delacey Skinner, then-president of the Southern Literature Council of Charleston, had become something of a writers' retreat. As I understood it, writers who had previously spent an evening or been entertained in the house included Dorothea Benton Frank, Anne Rivers Siddons, and Pat Conroy.

Surrounding the place were palmetto trees, tall grasses, and a few other gorgeous old homes. There must have been a zillion seabirds of varying types flitting about the rooftops and trees in the cooler-than-normal (for that time of year) ocean breeze.

Then, for me personally, there was the grand prize.

Stepping out of my upstairs bedroom and onto the deck, my immediate vista was the palm-dotted beach below me, Charleston's vast harbor stretching beyond, and aging Fort Sumter, positioned atop shoals in the center of the harbor.

I remember thinking, had I been in command of a single artillery battery—142 years earlier—I might have easily assisted Confederate Gen. P. G. T. Beauregard as I directed fire from the position of my upstairs deck (though again, the house did not yet exist at the time of the firing on Fort Sumter, April 12–13, 1861).

Had it been eighty or ninety years before the firing on Fort Sumter, I easily could have assisted S.C. Militia Gen. William Moultrie, who would have been behind his works a few hundred yards to my left, exchanging shots with the 250-plus guns of British Admiral Sir Peter Parker's Royal Navy task force out in the harbor.

Moultrie, of course, commanded the now-famous garrison—which included Lt. (future Gen.) Thomas Sumter, Maj. (future Gen.) Francis Marion, Sgt. William Jasper, and my own five-times great-grandfather, Capt. Thomas Woodward, who commanded a company of South Carolina Rangers on Moultrie's extreme left, thus helping thwart an attempt by Royal Marines to land on the island and seize the fort.

The twelve-plus-hour battle for Sullivan's began around 9 A.M. on June 28, 1776, when Parker's ships opened fire on the fort. But to Parker's surprise, many of the British shells struck and sank harmlessly into the soft palmetto logs of which the fort was then constructed.

Parker's ships, on the other hand (some of which ran aground on the same harbor shoals that Fort Sumter would be built on years later) were constructed of oak, which Moultrie's artillerists quickly shattered, sending deadly splinters into the unfortunate British sailors and Marines.

Today Fort Sullivan is named Fort Moultrie in honor of Moultrie, who was destined to become a major general in the Continental Army and a South Carolina governor. South Carolina will forever be known as The Palmetto State. And though I have yet to touch on Charleston's myriad other military connections, traditions, tales, anecdotes, and yes, forts, perhaps readers will now have a better understanding of why "the Holy City" might have dual meaning to any American who has worn the cloth of the United States.

Oh, and what has since been described as the "first decisive victory of American forces over the British Navy" during the American Revolution? South Carolina's battle for Sullivan's Island. ☽

Lee Gordon Brockington

☽

A Place Called Hobcaw

In the fall of 1983, a friend from Maryland was purchasing feral swine from Ossabaw Island, Georgia, for a living history farm. We'd recently met because we were both historians and he asked about a place he'd heard about on the South Carolina coast that had wild hogs. Somewhere in the back of my mind, I remembered siblings who'd attended the University of South Carolina talking about field trips to Hobcaw Barony in Georgetown County, not far from Pawleys Island. I made some calls and got an appointment with the research reserve's wildlife biologist and then asked my friend to stay at our family's beach house on Pawleys.

I rode in the middle of the bench seat in the biologist's pickup truck and as the two men talked about "omnivorous and ubiquitous" feral swine, I looked ahead and saw changing vistas of one hundred-year-old longleaf pine, freshwater ponds, cypress and palmetto swamps, abandoned rice fields along the river, maritime forest at the heart of a barrier island, and a five thousand-acre salt marsh called North Inlet estuary.

Unknowing, I asked, "How did USC come to own all this land?" The biologist, who worked for Clemson University, quickly responded that neither the university nor the state owned Hobcaw Barony. It was all privately owned by the Belle W. Baruch Foundation because of a gift of an extraordinary woman. Belle Baruch was the daughter of Bernard Baruch, the Wall Street financier, adviser to presidents and South Carolina native. The last owner of the 17,500-acre plantation, Belle envisioned an outdoor laboratory for colleges and universities. Before her death in 1964, she created a trust and named trustees to operate the land for the benefit of research and education in marine biology, forestry and wildlife. Clemson and USC had both established institutes and dedicated permanent staffs of research faculty to Hobcaw and gained state and national reputations in science fields.

That day we traveled nearly seventy-five miles of dirt roads searching for feral swine. The hogs are descendants of domestic stock, now appearing in forty-five of our fifty states and named a Federal Invasive Species because of the destruction they cause to the natural and man-built environment.

But I was distracted. Distracted by Mr. and Mrs. Baruch's home on a bluff overlooking Winyah Bay, and Belle's 1937 house and stable set amidst live oaks and holly trees, Spanish moss and winter rye grass. Rice mill ruins, four abandoned slave villages, and a 1910 schoolhouse for the children of the Baruch's twentieth-century black employees had me asking questions the biologist could not answer.

I ended that day's visit at the newly built public education center at the front gate. Exhibits and a film helped me understand the amazing diversity of environments that made Hobcaw a highly recognized science center. But it was Hobcaw's broad history that made me wonder about its untold stories. Here there had been Native American occupation and enslaved Africans, naval stores, indigo and tidal rice production, and important twentieth-century visitors. I had heard of Bernard Baruch because I grew up in Columbia and knew of his friend James F. Byrnes; I'd ridden with the Camden Hunt and knew that the town was Baruch's birthplace; but I'd never known that Hobcaw Barony existed as a microcosm of American history. Winston Churchill and President Roosevelt stayed at Hobcaw and the servants who attended their needs were still living.

I surprised myself with my last question to the staff. "Are you hiring?" I had a perfectly fine job as curator of education at Historic Columbia Foundation, hired after a Columbia College internship led me to those three house museums. But I could sense the untold social history waiting to be unraveled, decades at a time, from 1500 to the present. Though the center's administrator was polite and even encouraging, he told me there were no openings. "But stay in touch with us," he added. When I left Pawleys Island that November, I updated my resume and mailed an envelope to the Belle W. Baruch Foundation.

After several visits, the staff finally relented and agreed to let me work for no pay, perhaps testing my resolve to work at the research reserve. I asked to call it an internship, for the sake of my short resume, and they agreed. I got a place to live on the north end of Pawleys Island and to pay the $150-a-month rent, got a job at Anchor Inn Restaurant in Murrells Inlet. I reported to work at Hobcaw Barony on April Fool's Day, 1984.

Hobcaw means "between the waters." It sits at the southern end of the Waccamaw Neck and measures 27.4 square miles—making it four times bigger than Brookgreen Gardens and even larger than Manhattan. The property's appeal as an outdoor laboratory stems from its promised protection, allowing scientists to study natural coastal processes over the long term. Within Hobcaw's boundaries are every representative environment in South Carolina's coastal plain, what others typically call "the lowcountry." Those islands, forests, swamps, and ponds offer scientists a chance to compare and contrast data. Damaging storms like Hurricane Hugo in 1989, Charlie in 2004 and a tornado in 1999 do not delay research or ruin projects. Instead, they give researchers information about natural recovery from natural events.

Understanding the lowcountry also means studying the cultural history. The same year I began work for the foundation, Dr. Charles Joyner's *Down By the Riverside* was published, highlighting the history of the slave community on the Waccamaw Neck. Soon, Charleston-area scholars produced works on African-influenced sweetgrass baskets and McKissick Museum sent anthropologists into the field to conduct oral history interviews of slave descendants, many of whom still lived on lowcountry rice plantations. The National Park Service took a greater interest in the Gullah/Geechee history and named the southeastern coast from Jacksonville, North Carolina to Jacksonville, Florida "one of the ten most endangered places in America." The environment influences the culture, and the coast, developed and taken for granted as a tourist destination for so long, was quickly becoming a laboratory for greater understanding among the races, the classes and the struggle to reconcile the past.

And here is Hobcaw, a microcosm of history, an outdoor laboratory, an aid to cultural history researchers. The seasonal movement of coastal native Americans and their mysterious shell rings, shell mounds and shell middens, present at Hobcaw, yield unique information to USC archaeologists —middens made solely of clamshells and not oysters or a mix found elsewhere. Coastal Carolina University archaeologists searched for evidence of the first attempted European settlement in North America, believed to have occurred in 1526 on the eastern bank of Winyah Bay, which lies along Hobcaw's shores.

The Spanish arrived in August with six hundred settlers, but by October, the 150 survivors returned to Hispaniola, leaving the area to be fought over by the French and English.

By 1718, Hobcaw became a "barony," a land grant from the king of England to one of South Carolina's Lords Proprietors. By the late eighteenth century, Hobcaw Barony had been sold and subdivided into plantations.

Georgetown County grew more rice than any other place in the world, except for the area around Calcutta, India. One of the nation's largest slave owners owned a plantation carved from Hobcaw. Many of those slaves' descendants still lived on the land after emancipation.

At Hobcaw is the evidence of the owners' and slaves' lives, their family homes, their sources of food, methods of transportation, and based on oral histories, their desire—both whites' and blacks'—to leave or stay on the land. Change did not truly come until the early twentieth century when Bernard Baruch, by 1905 a wealthy Wall Street wizard, bought the contiguous plantations and reassembled the barony for use as a winter hunting retreat. He hired white men as superintendents and one hundred or so black men and women as duck guides, boat makers, horse handlers, dog trainers, ditch diggers, cooks, and maids.

Photographs taken during the Baruch era were in drawers and photo albums, while a few lined the exhibit hall. Home movies of duck hunting had been found and transferred to videotape and a short film had been made to chronicle the story of "Belle's Legacy." A cultural resource inventory had been done to identify artifacts and remains of the past and there it all was, waiting to be discovered, to be studied and put together like the pieces of a puzzle left in a grandmother's hall closet when I arrived in 1984.

One of the big pieces was Friendfield Village, one of the very few former slave villages still extant in the state and largely preserved because it was lived in until the 1950s. The Smithsonian's American History Museum came knocking, wanting one of the antebellum cabins for its new exhibit on slavery in the South. The trustees considered the gift and then voted to expand Belle's vision of research and education in the fields of marine biology, forestry and wildlife to include historic preservation. The cabin remains at Hobcaw and conservation of it and three other buildings in the village mark a significant change in how the past is viewed.

Foundation trustees and directors, scholars and architects had the skill and knowledge to preserve the past. But I like to think I provided a sense of timing and a voice for history. Ever since I was a child, I wanted to sit at the feet of great aunts and grandfathers, cousins in small towns and their maids and cooks "in the back." In my first museum workshops and seminars, I learned of the new social history, moving away from studying only great men and great events to studying ordinary people and everyday lives.

About the time I arrived at Hobcaw, that interest had caught the public's attention as well. By meeting former residents of the villages and the sons and daughters of white superintendents, many of whom still worked

Friendfield Church, rebuilt circa 1890, offered AME and Baptist services until about 1950 for residents of four former slave villages at Hobcaw Barony. Photograph by Jessica Bichler.

at Hobcaw or at nearby Pawleys, I had a chance to hear their voices and then perhaps to speak for them. Their poignant stories of meeting generals, congressmen, journalists, and movie stars were mingled with memories of dancing at the "big house" for tossed coins and watching alligators attack and drown a cousin while fishing.

The employees lived in houses with no electricity or running water, while Bernard and Belle both had houses with all the modern conveniences. They could see the contrast, but were happy to have a job during the Depression; working fourteen-hour days in heat and cold, but knowing a plantation doctor's office was open once a week. They were isolated on The Neck with no bridge to the mainland, but they could travel by the Baruchs' car, train, or plane when necessary.

These contrasts were easier for me to understand after I met Robert McClary, a descendant of slaves who grew up at Hobcaw and now lives near Detroit. Robert began to return to the plantation alone and then with siblings. In 2003, for the first time, he brought his mother. He was not the first person I'd met who asked permission to visit his childhood home and "take a look around," nor was he the first to bring his extended family. We'd hosted family reunions and honored requests for burials and funerals. But Robert was the most outspoken about his mixed emotions—a love/hate relationship with the south, with plantations of the twentieth century, with the sharp contrasts between rich and poor, black and white in his little corner of the world at Hobcaw.

In 1944, President Roosevelt stayed a month at Hobcaw and Robert got to meet his idol on the side of a dirt road on the plantation. When asked by the president, "What do you want to be when you grow up, little boy?" young Robert McClary answered, "Why I'd like to be president of the United States!" The president of the United States threw his head back and laughed a mighty laugh. Stung, Robert made up his mind to be somebody. Meeting Robert and his family, hearing his version of life at Hobcaw and knowing about his sense of the place changed me. My job as historian and interpreter of Hobcaw's history comes with a responsibility not only to scholars' research into Baruch and Roosevelt, but especially to those like Robert McClary, whose own life histories have been untold for so long. Southern history has long focused on the landowners and leaders of society, but the success of the south also rests in the labor of the overlooked people who worked hard, lived simply, but loved the land just as much.

Experiencing history through those who lived it, in the place where they lived it, is rare. Hobcaw remains a testament to the lives of slaves, who created the wealth of the rice culture, to the lives of the plantation owners whose descendants held on to the land for generations, and to Belle Baruch, whose concern for the environment and her love of "the friendliest woods in the world" led to its preservation in perpetuity. Who I am now, as a professional and a human being, is created largely by my experiences working here. Meeting international researchers, eating some of the best seafood in the world, leading tours and school field studies—all these experiences are tempered with the words of the former residents: "I am a part of this place. I mattered. I love this place."

This place is called Hobcaw Barony. ☽

Stephen Hoffius

)

Where God Is Courteous

Every once in a while, when I drive from my home in Charleston to either Beaufort or Savannah, which I sometimes do every week, I pull off of Highway 17 a couple of miles and drive to the old Sheldon Ruins. It's an historical mystery, a spiritual sanctuary, a free zone where people feel comfortable talking with strangers, even sharing stories of their grandparents and their mixed feelings about churches and religion. Sky-scraping oaks and pines rise to the heavens, tufts of moss sway in the breeze, thick vines swoop from branch to branch. And there in the middle of the clearing sits one of the great architectural achievements of the state, the ruins of Sheldon Church, the former Church of Prince William's Parish. Sheldon, like so many places in South Carolina, lies at the intersection of what was and what is and what might have been. It invites wonderment from all who visit.

It's just four brick walls, no roof, no windows or doorways, no pews or paneling or stained glass, but it's humbling and people who visit lower their voices.

The walls, three to four feet thick, rise about twenty feet above the ground. Openings mark where fourteen windows and doors once existed, including a massive fifteen-foot-wide arched window that towered above the pulpit. The earliest image of the church is a 1798 painting by Charles Fraser, and it was already ruined then, roofless, the windows empty-socketed.

The four brick columns still stand out front, though the pediment they once supported is long gone. Both of the church's long sides still support six engaged columns. Originally built about 1757, the building has been a ruin far longer than it was an active church. It has been called the "finest country church in America" and has stood up to Charleston's much more famous houses of religion. The design is that of a classic temple of ancient Greece

Sheldon Ruins.
Photograph by Jack Alterman.

or Rome. Scholars have claimed it is the first such structure ever built in America. And here it stands in what, with apologies to Beaufort County, is still pretty much the middle of nowhere.

It's South Carolina's Acropolis, our own Roman Colosseum.

Whatever stress I have in my life evaporates after a stroll around the grounds. I've looked over the fallen tombstones dozen of times, but I still read them and puzzle about what the building looked like in its prime, about the community that once surrounded it.

This was one of the centers of the South Carolina rice industry. The Bull family's five thousand-acre Sheldon plantation was next door, and the Bellingers' Tomotley isn't far away. According to Frederick Dalcho's *Historical Account of the Protestant Episcopal Church in South Carolina* (1820), "seldom less than 60 or 70 carriages, of various descriptions, were seen at the Church on the Lord's day." After the services, "the more respectable part of the congregation" was invited to Stephen Bull's nearby plantation, and everyone else to the home of Bull's overseer. The church was richly paneled and had square pews with benches across three sides, not unlike the pews at the Brick Church of St. James-Santee near McClellanville. On the door of the Bull family pew was engraved the family's coat of arms with the curious motto, "God Is Courteous." Not "God Is Great" or "All Powerful," but "God Is Courteous," as if He has good table manners and never picks His holy teeth.

At the rear of the church was a raised loft for the choir and organ, divided from the congregation by a wooden partition topped by red curtains so the parishioners couldn't peek in. A large baptismal font just inside the door was supported by bronze clawed feet. By the front entrance, according to some early accounts, stood a life-sized equestrian statue of Prince William, Duke of Cumberland, the son of King George II.

Only about thirty years after it was built, the place burned to the ground. The state historical marker by the road claims it was "Burned 1779 by British," but the arsonists weren't actually British. The credit or blame apparently goes to a Beaufort man named Andrew DeVeaux, who had originally supported the rebels' cause but then turned against his upstart country because his father, who supported the British, "may have received some harsh words, or other treatment, as a tory." Joseph Johnson's *Traditions and Reminiscences, Chiefly of the American Revolution in the South* (1851) goes on to describe DeVeaux as more of a mischievous imp than a traitor or warrior. "He united with a number of inconsiderate, frolicsome young men, and embarrassed the proceedings of the Whigs, whenever an opportunity occurred." DeVeaux's buddies apparently weren't as serious about their rebellion as he was, so he wanted to trick them into some act that would seal their ties to the British. "DeVeaux led his men there only to vex the rebels, as he told them; but when there, he induced them to ravage the [Sheldon] plantation, and burn Sheldon Church," Johnson continues. "There was no retracting from their allegiance after such an act."

So Sheldon Church, one of the great architectural structures of South Carolina if not the young nation, was torched as part of an act that sounds suspiciously like fraternity brothers egging each other on until someone tosses a rock through a window. "Boy, you done it now, Bubba." The statue of Prince William was thrown into the outhouse at the Bull plantation next door.

Thirty-six years later, in 1815, trees grew where pews had been built, but people in the area still determined to hold a service at Sheldon. So they cut down the trees and laid boards across the stumps. By 1826 the place was rebuilt and thriving. Twice the congregation raised $10,000 to restore it to its colonial glory, but before they got around to the full restoration another war swept through. In January 1865 the place was burned again, this time by U.S. General John Logan's troops.

However the church wasn't actually destroyed then. At the end of the Civil War it looked far better than it does today. In February 1866 a relative of the former minister wrote his mother, "Sheldon Church is not burnt down. It has been torn up inside somewhat but it could be repaired." In no time, however, the place was looted by locals. A few days later that same scribe penned, "I see fragments of Sheldon Church all about."

Nonetheless, the walls were still solid—for a while. Around the turn of the century a caretaker lived on the grounds. A 1922 article in the *Beaufort Gazette* claims that the walls and interior plaster "are in perfect repair. . . . Along the inside walls are still to be found tiny little marble shelves on which the candles which lighted up the building were placed."

No more. In the last ninety years most of the plaster has been stripped down to the brick, and the marble shelves have been removed. But the whole place remains in remarkably good shape. No more looting, no graffiti. Ferns sprout from the brick and mortar, but no trees grow in the interior. The garbage can that sat by the gate has been removed, but very little trash can be found on the ground. Visitors seem to respect the site. Every year, the second Sunday after Easter, an Episcopal service is put on for hundreds of parishioners.

It's a great place to visit anytime. I can personally attest to the fact that normally unruly dogs, when released from the cars that have imprisoned them, stroll reverently around the grounds, respecting the privacy of the other visitors, peeing on the bushes but not the holy bricks. Somehow they seem for once to learn their manners, maybe because, at least at Sheldon, God Is Courteous. And we who visit it are too. ☽

The Edisto Motel
The Great Falls of the Catawba
Tobacco Auctions
The Alston School
Glenn Springs Water
Daufuskie Oysters
Mary's Celebrity Supper Club
Bucksville
The Ocean Forest Hotel
Camp Wadsworth
The *Henrietta*
Asparagus Farms
Ellenton
The Carolina Parakeet
Krispy Kreme Deliveries
Rainbow Lake
The *Columbia Record*
The Oregon Hotel
Palmetto Park and Pond
The Hot and Hot Fish Club
Big Thursday
The Pad
Cogburn's
Truluck Vineyards
Pawleys Pavilion
"Bull Street"
Theodosia . . .

Gone

Remembering Keowee

The View Through the Bridge

Amazing, the images we've saved from childhood, the memories of this Pickens County countryside, in God's greenest valley. And always up front, there's the hole in the bridge.

It was a great thrill for kids to play in the cool shade of Chapman's covered bridge, across Keowee, at the lower end of the Eastatoee Valley.

First thing quite a few remember, after seventy years or so, is the terror of the hole in the floor. It was maybe a knothole rotted out, too small for even a toddler's foot to slip through. A hen's egg probably could not roll through it.

But under the juvenile eye, the frigid jade of that water rippled and rolled beneath us, swirling along fallen twigs and the rosy blooms of laurel from the woods upstream. It whispered in the voices of spirits, and what it sounded like was "Gonna git-chee! Gonna git-chee! Pull you through!" Or that is what older siblings interpreted.

Spirit voices, and no wonder.

This was the river that cut through the hills of what is now upland South Carolina, watering the homeplace of the Lower Cherokee Nation, nurturing in its deep woods, pools, and bottoms the wild fruits and birds, fishes and beasts of Eden. The river was called Keowee. (Keowee is supposed to have meant "place of the mulberries"—logical, because there were plenty of them. But, dubious, as so many Native "meanings" have been supplied by romantic novelists of pallid skin and distant backgrounds.)

Anyway, it was a fine place. "A fruitful vale," one explorer wrote, too enticingly. Word spread, and inevitably, indigenous locals came home from

Chapman's covered bridge (1917–1974).
Photo courtesy of Pickens County Library System.

the hunt one day to find their lodges in ashes, their fields of corn and squashes destroyed, and their families homeless and in hiding, if still among the living.

A real estate boom was about to begin.

Under British rule, in order to keep the tribe loyal to the crown, white occupation of Cherokee lands was forbidden—a rule that some scofflaw Colonials doubtless reveled in breaking. A few found a "legal" way around the ban, by marrying Cherokee women. A monument to such a union was, for centuries, the oldest known dwelling in the valley of Keowee, the Eastatoee home of trader James Beamer and his Cherokee family, built around 1740 and only recently destroyed.

With American independence came the floods of white people, as the Native tenants of that dying era departed. The first deeds for land up the Savannah headwaters, of which Keowee was prime, were recorded in 1784. New communities grew along the river, as the buffalo and clouds of lavishly colored green birds, the Carolina parakeets, bit the dust.

Because of the size of the sprawling tracts newcomers bought, or claimed, next-door neighbors could be miles away. But they were the neighbors, nonetheless. They cleared (at first) small plots of land, used the massive timber to build their homes—one such roomy, two-story domicile is still remembered as "the five-log house"—married the neighbors' daughters, and birthed swarms of children who would never know, nor covet, any other home.

These were my people, the ancestors of my parents, the kin that claimed a river-washed landscape for several dozen miles. They "lived at home"— their way of saying they made their crops, raised their stock, made everything they needed, offered neighborly help when trouble struck on any side, and devoted not one tittle of their brains nor energy to "public work"—a quietly disapproving term for trading the hours of one's life to a businessman for pay.

In its earliest days of development the land watered by Keowee was part of the Ninety Six District. That is, the courthouse that served a vast stretch bordered by the upper Savannah was in the trading and military outpost town of Ninety Six, so named because it lay ninety-six miles down the Cherokee Path from the Lower Cherokee capital, Keowee Town, and its neighboring British military stockade, Fort Prince George.

With the growing population, and not all of these new citizens being parsons or prim schoolmarms, transporting prisoners to court in Ninety Six became a major chore, as punishing to the lawman as to the captive—who, uplander that he was, held a determined and fleet-footed love of liberty. So in the 1790s a new court district was formed in Pendleton. And when that facility was outgrown, in 1826 a spot on Keowee, on a trafficky Cherokee-made path, now South Carolina Highway 183, became the site of Pickens Courthouse. It would be the seat of justice from the Saluda River on the east to Chattooga River on the west, till after the Civil War.

Open to the thrills of technology, the champions of this new town bought into what seemed a fine idea. Steamboats were all the rage. If workers could blast a channel up Seneca River from Hamburg, on the Savannah, and on up Keowee into the mountains, the profits could be amazing.

Tourists were enduring bumpy, hot, and dusty carriage rides to reach the cooler heights of the Blue Ridge. Whiskey-makers upriver were having to raft their brimming kegs downstream to Hamburg and beyond, with mishaps possible along the way. Cotton would be king, but not until there was a better way to haul it to the mills than rafts and mule trains. An inland port at Pickens would solve so many things!

So when the new log Pickens Courthouse was built, in the 1820s, on a rise above the river, it was set to face downstream, the better to see the steamboat churning toward its berth, whistle blasting, upscale passengers crowding the rails.

It never happened. Thwarted by a submerged plateau of solid granite, encountered somewhere down near Anderson, the channel diggers withdrew. The crowded wagon road would just have to do.

The village of Pickens Courthouse grew and bustled. Built on an orderly grid of lots, it became home to several hundred, who educated their children at an academy and found entertainment at a theater and an occasional hanging. Eventually the Presbyterians built an austere little red brick church.

Then came the tragedy of civil war, and in its aftermath, another territorial split. In 1868, the Pickens District was divided: Everything west of Keowee River, to the Georgia line at Chattooga River, became the new Oconee County, with the German Colonization Society settlement of Walhalla its new county seat. Pickens County, on the east side of the river, made itself a seat of government in what became the new town of Pickens, some fourteen miles east of Keowee, and about halfway to the new county's eastern border, on the Saluda. In those days, a courthouse nailed the core of a community to the globe, assuring merchants, lawyers, doctors, schoolmarms, and migrating citizens at large that "settling in" was safe—at least, till the court district grew again to the splitting point.

The emigrating citizens of the town of Pickens Courthouse picked up their belongings, often including their houses, and moved one way or the other. Soon there was very little left, except the returning forest, and the river's rocky song, as it rounded the base of the hill beside the church and cemetery.

For a while, people returned to hold services at the church. Some came on the river, in the little boats they called "bateaus." When the Presbyterians stopped sending a preacher, after a while the Methodists took up the cause. In 1886, the shock of the deadly Charleston earthquake came up the rivers, and cracked the brick walls in a couple of places, visible still today.

Back a couple of years, early in the twenty-first century, I was with a group of young school children visiting Old Pickens Presbyterian Church. In recent years its survival has been highlighted by a team of Clemson University historians who are mapping the old settlement. Most of the site is now covered by the vast network of Duke Energy operations surrounding the Oconee Nuclear Station.

In my own childhood, in the cemetery there was a broken crypt over a baby's grave. Though the grave itself was securely underground, we used to peep in the ruined end of the vault, sure that in its darkness there were bones. Well, here again after seventy years, the first thing the school kids discovered was that cracked little crypt. In all these years, neither the grave nor kids' enthralled curiosity has changed a bit.

My grandmother, who played the organ at the church, died young and was buried at the foot of a massive chestnut tree nearby—an ephemeral marker that perished in the 1940s, in the chestnut blight. She left four children, the oldest a girl then eleven, and three boys, who were then nine, five, and an infant. My father, the five-year-old, recalled his mother's burial in characteristically few words. "I stood there and watched that red clay shoveled down on that coffin, and nobody even held my hand." Life was turning grim.

Though their mother's family were people of material substance, the children's father refused their help. He was unable to cope, himself, and the raising of that little family fell to the only girl. She and the brothers old enough to use a hoe worked people's corn and cotton fields. They fished the river and hunted far and wide in the near-endless miles of woods. The caregiver treated injuries and ailments with whatever was on hand—grease for burns, yellowroot for sore throats, a tea of what she called "Rat Vein," wintergreen, for stomach ills, and boiled squirrel brains for ailments not quite diagnosed.

On a hunting expedition, my father, then about twelve, shinnied through a fence, caught the trigger of his shotgun on the wire, and shot off three of his fingers. There was nothing to do but wrap his hand in a rag, and walk to the nearest doctor, some ten miles. After the doctor sewed up the remains of that hand, he tried to put the child to bed at his house. But no, the boy would not stay, because he knew his sister would be terrified when he did not come home. So he made his thanks, and set out for the walk back home.

The baby, who sat in the crop rows while the other children worked, ate so much grass that he was suffering a near-fatal intestinal blockage when his sister carried him to a relative for help. That was the "in" the kin were waiting for. They kept him for five years or more, which he remembered, always, as the happiest time of his ninety years of life.

Despite everything, that sister sent those boys to school. They went as far as the community school could take them—through the seventh grade. Only the baby went to college.

Lots more water went under the bridge for my family on Keowee. My father and mother ran away and married, in 1922, and could never live on Keowee again. So all I know of it is as a childhood visitor, and the bearer of their ever-homesick tales. We were always "going home" but I was the only one who made it.

This morning I cooked breakfast in the cast iron skillet that my daddy's sister used. I remember the abundance of her house in her later years, the pie safe full of biscuits, slab meat and fried pies, the crocks of pickled beans and pickled pork and kraut, the cotton wagon we rode in to the field, where they let me pretend to help them pick. When the lady died, quite old, I thought it was so nice that the undertaker drove the hearse, followed by a procession of cars, the long way around to the churchyard, so that she would pass by Keowee one last time. Not long after, Keowee River died too.

In 1965, Duke Power announced its planned Keowee-Toxaway project. It would dam the river in two places over the next five years, creating a lower lake called Keowee, and another, Jocassee, upriver. Lake Jocassee would inundate the valley of Jocassee, much of Keowee's headwaters of Toxaway River and Whitewater River and lands adjoining.

The Keowee Dam grew beside the long abandoned village of Old Pickens, backing water over where my people (and lots of others) used to farm, over the relics and Cherokee burial sites of Keowee Town, over the remnants of Fort Prince George, over history.

The dam at Jocassee covered the way of life of a self-sustaining mountain people. It drowned a tourist haven, whose principal hotel, divers have discovered, remains much as it was, now in the icy dark three hundred feet under the breathtakingly gorgeous waters.

The river that was once everybody's playground, and the sustenance of many, died to make electricity for people hundreds, thousands of miles away, and lakefront homesites for those who could afford them. Moved to cross a narrow finger of the lake, Chapman's Bridge and the hole in its floor burned, in the 1970s. Old Pickens Church stands firm and is used, occasionally. Probably the most opulent of the village's moved buildings, the Hagood-Mauldin House, is a lovingly kept museum in downtown Pickens. Another, once at the site of the Keowee Dam, the Pleasant Alexander House, is now the office at High Falls County Park, in Oconee County.

Far more than human communities along Keowee have taken new shape, wrought by "progress." The Scots-bred ancients of my own tribe loved a good old stewpot of eel, seined readily from dooryard streams. No more— eel offspring, born in the Sargasso Sea, can only swim so far back up their

The author reflects on what lies beneath Lake Keowee on Highway 11, about three miles downriver from where Chapman's Bridge once spanned the Keowee River between Pickens and Oconee counties. Photograph by Kate Gavenus.

parents' rivers, before the dams block them forever. Conversely, beavers, in any appreciable number, had been missing for generations, until the new lakes made their travels so much easier. Now many a pond and swamp has evolved in once-dry woods and fields.

Invisible is the soul change, the shadow of elders' loss drifting over the vast acres and miles of new, crystal aquamarine that once was Keowee.

From the Highway 11 bridge, looking out on it for the first time, after the dams did their work, it was surreal. In shock I said to it, "All that we thought we were, all that we thought we had, the aspirations, the labor, our history—all that lies under where I stand. You are a sea of ghosts." ☽

)

Blackberries for BMWs

Growing up in Spartanburg County, I learned the meaning of bittersweet by battling the brambles that grew alongside our tar-and-gravel country roads. Neither snake nor sticker could keep my scratched and scrawny arms from reaching through into the briar-laden gullies to pluck up the blackberries that grew so abundantly there. Seedy, and often concealing tiny spiders and grit within the purple pockets of juice, there was no reliable way to tell whether the sun-warmed fruit, once popped into a hungry mouth, would yield sweet honey nectar or the caustic bitterness of a sour berry. Such was life on the edge of the woods and so deep in the county that you had to live there to know where you were.

The baby girl in a family of boys who preferred hot rods and rock music to spending time with their little sister, I lived the life of an only child. Our small, brick ranch house was so far out in the country it was on the way to nowhere. I found my playground in the gnarly roots of hardwood trees, my playmates custom designed from my imagination. Wild plums that grew wormy, but succulent in copses down the dirt road toward the pond, were morning and afternoon snacks. Arts and crafts consisted of mud pies, adorned with pebbles and acorn caps, patted smooth and left to dry in the merciless South Carolina sun.

Horizons were created by longleaf and loblolly pines that grew of their own accord and stood sentinel, blocking the winds at the back of cotton and soybean fields. Field trips were bike rides taken alone, but never lonely, down an unthreatening road to Mr. and Mrs. Waddell's country store. The couple, both always present, greeted me like a friend, and twenty-five cents bought a party that would last an entire afternoon. Airplanes that flew overhead, landing and lifting off at the airport nearby where my father

The author in 1968 on a garden tractor outside her grandparents' home in Greer. Photo courtesy of Cynthia Boiter.

worked, represented more than unknown other places—they represented other worlds created wildly and without reservation in my young and untethered mind.

Apart from the constant dynamism of the natural world, the only things that changed on the stage of my childhood were the seasons, and they did so subtly and with little ruckus in typically southern fashion. Our little corner of Spartanburg County, back in the 1960s, was a study in consistency.

Like many children of the south, I grew up and grew away from my home—southern roots stretching into infinity as they do. My parents moved into the suburbs and I moved on to college, marriage, and a home and family of my own in another part of the state. I journeyed back to the piney forests and wandered along the kudzu-encroached roads of my childhood only in my memories, taking for granted that I would be able to find them safely where I had left them forever.

But everything I had come to believe about the constancy of the artifacts and vestiges of my youth changed in 1992 when a German automotive company announced they would be building a multi-million-dollar assembly plant on the land where cotton, soybeans, and hundreds of bare-foot, honeysuckle-sipping children once grew. Employing thousands of workers, way had to be made, both for the facility itself and the thousand some-odd surrounding acres it demanded.

Suddenly, a forty-year-old, three-bedroom Masonite house in need of plumbing repairs and a new roof but with a sweet little strawberry patch out back increased in worth exponentially. No longer needed to shelter families or provide backdrops to the rituals of life good country people had enjoyed—spring gardens, watermelon slicing, and shade tree sitting, to name a few—our former homes suddenly claimed an unheard-of value that could only be realized in their absence.

Value and worth are tricky concepts.

For people whose lives had been lived with poverty hovering near them like a not-so-distant relative, the value of money and land was a concept played with fast and loosely in Spartanburg County in the 1990s. It seemed that everyone would come out on top. One of our neighbors, a beautician by trade, jumped at the offer of $1.3 million for the sale of her house and parlor and yard where her daughter and I had once jumped like grasshoppers in the back of a two-ton truck full of itchy, just-picked cotton. It was a deal. But another neighbor signed away his land just as quickly before realizing that the cemetery where everyone in his family was buried, dating to the 1860s, would go the way of the bulldozer as well.

My own grandparents had no choice but to leave their home and with it the dirt floor of the barn where generations of kittens had hidden from generations of overly affectionate children, and put down their eighty-plus-year-old roots in a gently used suburban tract house. With the money they had left from the sale of the place where my cousins and I had grown up hunting Easter eggs, playing Red Rover, and stealing our grandpa's little green apples, they bought new furniture—a dining room suite and a couple of La-Z-Boy recliners.

Such is the way of the great industrial dialectic; there is much to be gained from progress, but quite a bit of paradise can be lost along the way. My old stomping ground is not the first pleasant place in somebody's memory to give way to the inevitable. Something or somebody once grew where virtually every building in this country stands. As a child, I would go for Sunday afternoon car rides with my father as he pointed out beloved places from his past already surrendered to concrete: the ghosts of old homeplaces, open fields full of promise from his memories. Today I can do the same with my daughters and before long they'll do the same with theirs.

The poet e. e. cummings told us that progress can be a comfortable disease. But it doesn't have to be without conscience. By all accounts, the new residents at my old homeplace are doing right by the environment they now inhabit; as far as manufacturers go, their sustainability record is admirable. But the bittersweet reality is that a precious and fertile part of the county has now gone fallow except for the production of American-made German automobiles. So I can't help but wonder if the good people at BMW might find a spot, somewhere amid the concrete and the asphalt, for a little plaque telling something about what was previously produced on those 1,150 acres. Blackberries, plums, memories, and children—and all of them growing wild. ☽

The Groins

Long, long ago (twenty-five years) on a planet far, far away (Washington, D.C.) I was searching in vain for an exit from the National Archives Building. I can't recall why I was there, only that I been unsuccessful, and was in retreat. And then a door opened at random onto the archivists' coffee room. There they were, at least a half-dozen librarians attending to their coffee cups. Yet they made me welcome. What were my interests? Pretty much anything. Where was I from? The coast of South Carolina. Just north of Charleston. McClellanville, a fishing village on the shores of the Cape Romain National Wildlife Refuge.

Then it was in the elevator, down, down, down, and along one corridor and then another and I was being shown the complete federal records of the Cape Romain National Wildlife Refuge. This sixty-four thousand acres of barrier islands, bays, creeks, and marshes had been assembled in the 1930s and still today this place of wild beauty is one of the most productive nesting areas for shorebirds and loggerhead turtles (and famed as well for spottail bass fishing and plain old beachcombing). The Promised Land. My father, William P. Baldwin Jr., had been a Junior Refuge Manager at that refuge. He'd arrived in 1938, thrown himself into the work with the passion of a wildlife biologist true believer and stayed with the government seventeen years. And here, wonder of wonders, were his reports to his bosses, the main one being the fabled J. Clark Salyer. And here were Salyer's replies and Salyer's other correspondence—including semi-secret inner office memos. The Fish and Wildlife Service was in its infancy. The Cape Refuge was only a decade old and just four years into an extensive expansion that centered on the newly acquired Bulls Island—where my father had worked and sometimes lived. I sat and read for four straight days, took notes and made copies and went home with the notion of writing a book-length history of the Cape Romain Wildlife Refuge.

I wrote and wrote and wrote. My New York agent found a very good publisher. An advance was in the works. Big money. "Six Square Miles!" That was the title chosen by my agent. "It's sixty square miles," I explained in vain. "The sound," he replied. "The sound."

Then I wrote some more and some more and began to have nightmares, ones where my agent was slicing into my brain. In short, I'd discovered things about my father's efforts as a wildlife biologist that were difficult to celebrate—difficult to even face. I dropped the project. And now, twenty-five years later, I'd like to explain why. I'll start with the "Groins" chapter.

In early 1936, plans were finished for the 1,800-foot-long Jack's Creek dike on the north end of Bulls Island and the Army Corps of Engineers was requested to begin the work by using one of their dredges to pump in material. Plans also were being drawn for a small dike to be built on the north end of Cape Island. But the Jack's Creek dike had top priority—and immediately entered a crisis mode. Once the marshlands had been left the dike was to continue for a short distance on the lower portion of the highland. And there directly in its plotted path was a low octagonal structure of oyster shell tabby. Known locally as "the Spanish fort," the thirty-foot-wide obstacle had not even been a matter of consideration until Deputy Manager Moore's father wrote a letter to the editor of the Charleston newspaper in protest and brought on the unfortunate attention of the public. Salyer chided Moore, whose father had caused "needless embarrassment and confusion." There was no proof that the "alleged" fort had historical significance. If it had Moore should have said so sooner, especially since it was Moore's route that the dike was following. The dike would go on as planned. The fort would be covered, and in the future Moore and his family members would clear their publications with the Fish and Wildlife Service.

That was a curiously hard line to be taking, for though records were almost nonexistent, the structure was probably a 1704 lookout post put there to keep an eye on invading Spanish and French and marauding pirates who liked to use the Jack's Creek anchorage. And in the wars since it had been used as a fort by whoever came along. And strangest of all, to shift the dike either left or right thirty feet would have raised no problems. A matter of principle. After eleven months of visits from interested historical groups, the plans for the "alleged fort" were officially changed. Salyer's Washington assistant, A. C. Elmer, wrote the regional administrant in Atlanta, James Silver, to tell him to tell Binks DuPre, my father's first real boss, that "under no circumstances must these old fortifications be destroyed in the completion of the Jack's Creek Dyke."

Salyer to Elmer to Silver to DuPre: a somewhat shaky chain of command was in place. Moore was gone by then. His superiors had not been happy with his managerial abilities. He had difficulty directing the mushrooming work force and could not get along with the new engineer, Captain Egoroff. The engineer, a White Russian immigrant, had come to the island to direct the efforts of the CCC crews now housed there. They would stop the erosion on the front of Bulls Island by building the earlier proposed set of groins. But not to protect the bird nesting areas as Salyer first suggested, but to keep the advancing ocean from breaking through into the new fresh water impoundment at Jack's Creek. The Russian engineer clashed with Moore.

"In the presence of the inspector," the report read, "Mr. Moore and Captain Egoroff became involved in a very heated argument on the present scheme of receiving mail on the Island." The deputy manager had not put up a mailbox as instructed and procrastinated in several other matters. It was advised that Moore be stripped of his authority. The mailbox incident was not the cause of Moore's problems, only the final incident. All the Refuge work could be handled by Manager DuPre, operating from McClellanville. Engineer Egoroff was doing "an excellent job in halting the erosion."

My father, who had arrived on Bulls Island by then, was in sympathy with Moore. Forty years later, he'd occasionally make a laughing reference to "the mad Russian" and shake his head. "The mailbox. Moore wanted it at the head of the road and the Russian wanted it at the end of the road." Captain Egoroff had an exasperating habit of meddling in the affairs of others, and even insisted on discussing my father's turkey management at a staff meeting. In general, he attempted to run the island. By June of 1936, however, Captain Egoroff was not a laughing matter to his Washington superior, Salyer. The groins project had by then taken on apocalyptic proportions and the entire island was threatened with deforestation.

Using his CCC crews, Egoroff had first built sandbag groins along the critical northernmost shore. These had been covered quickly by sand the bags raised and the sand continued to build. Satisfied with this the engineer had then begun to construct wooden groins using timber that had been cut along the island's newly made fire lines. The road to the beach was improved to aid in this construction and a sawmill was to be built to cut the planking for the groins.

The engineer had some definite ideas on beach erosion. An exact beach slope of a one-foot drop to every ten feet was to be maintained and the area around the groins was to be kept clear of debris, which meant that the numerous stumps that were continually working out of the beach sand (the forest of the preceding decade) must be kept cut down below the level of the beach sand. A year later this operation alone was occupying half of the CCC crews on a full-time basis, because each day more stumps would be revealed to be cut again. If the project failed it was because Egoroff's combined defenses of sandbags, hay bales and half-finished groins were not being cared for properly by the island's personnel. Having left the island for a short period, he wrote to Washington that the personnel must watch the hay bales after each high tide during daylight. During rough weather they must inspect them at night with flashlights. All washouts must be repaired at once. The existing groins must be braced when necessary. Clean the slope, fill the sandbags, remove the bark from the logs and prepare to operate the sawmill as soon as possible. That was the engineer's request.

As noted, Salyer had been enthusiastic about the groin project and readily agreed to buy the sawmill, which operated by the CCC would pay for itself. It was first estimated that the timber taken from the newly constructed fire lanes would be sufficient. But once the engineer returned and began to construct the groins it was found necessary to cut more. How much more? In the spring of 1938, Salyer was angered to find that no estimate could be made because no complete plans for the groins existed. But Egoroff insisted some plans and specifications did exist.

With still no telephone connection for the Refuge, Salyer telegraphed word that "agricultural engineering has seriously questioned major aspects of the work." Timber cutting was to be halted and an estimate made of the expected needs. Eight groins would use up to a half-million board feet. Two hundred thousand had already been cut. Plans had been made to use the mature trees and the forest survey indicated that the groins as drawn would take every tree taller than twenty-one inches on the island. Forty-two were called for. Placed every two hundred feet these structures were to run from eight feet above the mean high tide to mean low. And these would require 2 1/2 million board feet. By now, though, that estimate was irrelevant.

An engineer from the bureau's Agricultural Division had come to the island to examine Egoroff's work. And he had made two serious complaints. One, the groins were not strong enough to survive a severe storm. And two, since they were made from untreated lumber, marine worms were already eating away at the most seaward end. The whole would not last more than five years. It was decided that the eight started would be completed and used for study purposes. They would continue to keep the beach clean of driftwood and stumps and sand fences would be put along the north end of the island. In addition, the CCC crews would clean up the mess left by the timbering of the forest and new trees would be planted. In the future, Fish and Wildlife Service personnel would mark the trees to be cut.

Soon after this directive was made, high spring tides washed over the groins and broke into the new pond in two places. Egoroff reported eight to ten million gallons of salt water entered. He insisted that two more short tapering groins be placed at the end of the island. An additional sixty-one thousand board feet were cut. But the Russian engineer's part in the project was ending, and his duties were being transferred to the Agricultural Engineers. But the erosion methods of stump cutting and sloping were continued and a secondary dike was considered, a dike that would parallel the ocean and keep out the salt water. Finally asked his opinion, Manager Binks DuPre wrote that such a dike would not survive a severe hurricane and he had doubts about the two dikes already constructed. As for the groins, he did not think those built would survive more than thirty minutes "in a blow of that kind," and he was certain they would not build the beach higher than it was. Possibly they might stabilize it, but this "would be a subject for future correspondence."

But there was to be no future correspondence concerning the worth of groins. A small worm-eaten sample of one was mailed north and that project, as well as the cutting off of the stumps, was halted. On December 5, 1938, a telegram arrived announcing that a second dike well in from the beach and paralleling it would be built to keep the ocean out of the Jack's Creek pond. All other erosion work was to immediately stop. As to hurricane damage: the Hurricane of 1940 did punch a hole in the new second dike but except for a few pines weakened and killed by pine beetles, there was no real damage done. However, the beach behind the groins was completely swept away and the groins almost completely exposed. By 1942 marine worms had completely eaten away the seaward half of each. Soon they had vanished completely, and visitors today will find only the famed Bulls Island Boneyard, a picturesque assemblage of graying tree trunks and roots awash at high tide by the ocean waves.

The site of the groins is well to the seaward.

"The Government," my father would say. "Boondoggles . . . the Government." He stayed with the Fish and Wildlife Service for seventeen years and

Boneyard beach on Cape Romain.
Photograph by Robert Clark.

then went out on his own. My father was personable, charming. All said it. And very smart and in those younger days, very driven.

A couple years back the Fish and Wildlife director in Atlanta sent word he was publishing all my father's early reports—loggerhead turtle nesting, vegetation studies, deer trapping and turkey trapping. In the years since no one had written with such enthusiasm about the Cape Romain Refuge, or any other refuge I would guess. All very successful efforts except the last. The trapping of the turkeys had been his undoing. He inherited the turkey program. He was to finish trapping off the current Bulls Island turkeys because they were tainted with domestic fowl. Then he was to go into the mainland's Francis Marion Forest and trap all wild replacements, release them on the island, and their descendants would be trapped and sent to various parts of the state where wild turkeys were no longer found. He did this.

But there were ticks on the island, ticks so thick that the army would use it as a site to test insect repellant during World War II. The ticks would latch onto the necks of the turkeys, sometimes in the hundreds, and kill them. My father (perhaps with help from others) decided that the solution was to spray the island with DDT. World War II came and went. As he had only one lung my patriotic father stayed on as Senior Refuge Manager. The war over, his first assignment was to do a test survey of the effects of DDT on songbirds of the island. There'd been a test elsewhere showing a negative result. My father's yearlong study showed an increase in songbirds. That much was in the National Archive records. In my father's own paperwork for the study I found a memo, a 1946 memo from Washington, saying something like this: "Baldwin be careful with this. There's convincing proof that DDT interrupts the reproductive cycle of some shorebirds." Plans to spray the island from the air with DDT continued to be made. At that point I gave up all attempts to complete the book.

But then last month I was wandering through the stacks of the Charleston Library Society. That's the oldest library in America. The shelving system predates the Dewey Decimal System by a couple of centuries. I browsed the shelves. And there at my fingertips was a fairly new biography of Rachel Carson, whose book *The Silent Spring* had brought an end to DDT use in the United States. Small world. Carson had been the Fish and Wildlife Service public relations woman during my father's tenure. I flipped the pages. Having made enough money from a seashore book, she had retired from government service in 1952. In that same year she was in Myrtle Beach exploring the coastline. I know she came to Bulls Island one time. Likely this was it.

"1952. That's the year they gave up on trying to spray the island from a plane. They decided not enough poison would fall through the treetops." That was my father's explanation for halting the project. The Carson biography makes reference to Carson's field notes. They are up there in New England somewhere. I could find them. Will there be a meeting between this woman and my father?

My father died in 1993. I love him, his memory at least. And the older I get the more sympathy I have for him and for the human condition in general. I'll save that Rachel Carson investigation for the next life—or as Refuge Manager Binks DuPre would have it, "Make that a subject for future correspondence." ☽

The Upper Broad River

A Pastoral

Every time I drive I-85 north toward Charlotte and cross the Broad River near Gaffney I look downstream and think, "Cherokee Ford and 99 Islands." Before Duke Power dammed the Broad in the early part of the twentieth century, the river was storied territory, and I've always wanted to paddle it. There was an ancient river crossing at Cherokee Ford where Revolutionary War soldiers waded back and forth before two of the great battles of the war. Gold miners roamed the ridges and creek valleys looking for riches. An ironworks even operated at Cherokee Ford in the early nineteenth century. Then an early industrialist captured the falling water for power, and made a textile fortune.

Over spring break several years ago I finally took a three-day canoe trip down that section of the Broad with my friend Venable Vermont. Venable, Spartanburg-born and raised, has lived in Alaska since 1983. Before he retired from his day job as an attorney, he spent weekends and summer vacations paddling, hunting, hiking, and climbing over as much wild country as he could get his arms around.

He hasn't forgotten his roots. Once a year Venable flies back to the south and turkey hunts with his brother John. He still misses the southern river swamps, and so a few years ago he brought back an acorn from a South Carolina swamp chestnut and planted it in his greenhouse. It grew taller than 6 feet and pushed against the roof, reaching for northern sky.

Once while I visited Venable in Alaska he and his wife Kim drove my wife and me downtown. The city of Anchorage sits in a bowl. In a state twice the size of Texas, Anchorage accounts for almost half the population, two hundred thousand souls, and a sprawl of buildings surrounded by a profound uplift of peaks. Look around and it's a 360-degree feast: the Alaska Range to the north, the Chugach Mountains to the east, and the mountains of the Kenai Peninsula to the south.

We discovered Anchorage is a study in contrasts. The highway leading downtown is wall-to-wall contemporary Americana: Blockbuster Video, Home Depot, fast food and fast retail. But then something jars you back four thousand miles north and you realize you're not "outside" (what the locals call the Lower 48) anymore. A few blocks from the central city we saw a cabin where someone still lives with moose skulls covering the roof.

Once in the central city Kim pointed out a line of ugly buildings along 3rd Avenue, a main drag hit very hard by the '64 earthquake: "You know, up here there's a ban on architecture. If you're an architect you can't come to Alaska."

If I lived in Alaska I'd probably choose Anchorage. It's a place, unlike most cities, that encourages you to believe the human world is puny and temporary. That's a lesson we need more in the world today. Being southern we tend to think in terms of established human patterns. Not always so in Alaska. The dew's still on the world up there, even in a city like Anchorage.

The dew's not on the Broad River, but it didn't dry long ago. We started in North Carolina in the shadow of White Oak Mountain. The first day we paddled the Green River, camped there, and the second day floated toward South Carolina and spent the night camped just above the South Carolina line. Venable had paddled part of the Green and the upper Broad with Scouts in the 1960s, but it was all new river for me. The best I could claim was that I had scouted some of the stretches from bridges.

It was a perfect weekend for paddling. But what is perfection on a river? Silence and pace of the journey have something to do with it, as does the way your eyes adjust to the little things—a hatch of small dark flies on the river's surface, or a silver stick bobbing in the current, a mottled trillium ready to open on the sandy bank, or the way the gray ghosts of gneiss outcrops on wooded slopes appear suddenly from the shadows and disappear again into the creases of the landscape as you pass. Perfection on a river is all around you.

In Cherokee County the Broad River passes under I-85's great asphalt ribbon just outside Gaffney. "Every time I drive over I look both ways and imagine floating under," I said as we passed under.

"I'll bet you're in the minority," Venable said. "Most people don't notice they're crossing a river these days."

There were several other bridges in the next few miles. The Southern Railroad Bridge downstream from the I-85 crossing is a beautiful WPA design, like a Roman aqueduct seen from the river. There's a stone abutment just below for an older bridge, and farther down is the crossing for U.S. Highway 29, a modern highway bridge. Sometimes from the river, the whole world looks like a ruin.

Past all the bridges is the site of Cherokee Ford, an ancient crossing of an Indian trail and one of the most important fords during the American Revolution. Warring forces on both sides crossed and recrossed the river there before and after the battles of Kings Mountain and Cowpens.

"The river at the ford is about 800 yards wide, and upon the firm pathway, which has been constructed at considerable expense, the average depth of water did not exceed one foot," wrote Benson J. Lossing in his 1850 *Pictorial Field Book of the Revolution Vol. II.* "Unless the river is much swollen, the ford is perfectly safe. A strong dam, owned by the proprietors of the iron works, crosses the river an 8th of a mile above; and so shallow and rapid is the current, and so rocky the bed of the river, for many miles in this vicinity, that it is quite unnavigable, except in a few places."

A little more than a mile downstream from the ford is Cherokee Falls, one of the early mill villages of the South Carolina upcountry. In the early nineteenth century there was a large ironworks there, but in 1881 a mill was first constructed with northern capital and know-how. Before that, as Bobby Gilmer Moss reports in *The Old Iron District*, his history of Cherokee County, "the waters of the Broad River ran practically unchecked to the sea."

The mill at Cherokee Falls harnessed the power of what has been described as "the cataract" of Cherokee Falls. The developers of the mill created industry in the midst of thousands of acres of what was once forest for feeding local iron furnaces. "Except for distillers, charcoal burners, and squatters," Moss writes, "the vast acres of the iron companies' forest lands were practically untenanted." The mill prospered until a fire destroyed it in 1894. It was so fierce it could be seen from Gaffney, four miles distant. After the fire the factory was rebuilt even bigger and prospered until the collapse of southern textiles in the late twentieth century.

Now the windows of the mill are boarded as the building awaits the fate of almost all the old factories—demolition and salvage. Very few of the old brick structures have been reused after the fickle finger of industry

Cherokee Falls on the Broad River, 1999.
Photograph by Mark Olencki.

abandoned much of the piedmont. Many like me wonder if once the mills go, can it be long in geologic time before the old dams disappear as well. We can only hope.

Approaching Cherokee Falls dam, it's hard to figure out a way to portage. There are no signs pointing the way. Burlington Industries, the owner of the mill in 1989, must not have followed through with the portage path reported on a fancy Duke Energy interpretive plaque we'd seen upstream. Or maybe the next owners abandoned the river trail or never finished it.

The only way around the odd, wide, multi-angle dam is to hug the right bank and work down to where the structure abuts the rocky shore. We took out, moved gear around the abutment and the exposed rock, which was dark and slippery, and slipped back in the river.

Cherokee Falls is significant because it's the first old cotton mill we've seen along the Broad. For one hundred years industry prospered in this isolated, dramatic Cherokee County spot. Now there's a big "for sale" sign on the mill's side. There is no industry here except for a few recreationists like us—either fishing or paddling.

Once we got a good view of the dam we could see how terribly it had deteriorated. There were once "batter boards" on top, a wooden skirt designed to bring up the pond level three or four feet above the concrete structure. Many of the boards were missing on the eight-foot dam. A gap in them about halfway across the river provides some thrills for area white-water boaters. I've seen videos on the Internet of local kayakers running the flume of water pressing through the broken dam. There would be none of that for us and our laden canoe, though below the Cherokee Falls dam there are big, long shoals that offer some good whitewater waves for surfing.

We ate lunch on the concrete dam abutment. Afterward we planned to pack the canoe and paddle down through the exciting shoals below. I couldn't finish my sandwich. I was nervous about the shoals. Before lunch I'd scouted the long broken ledge between us and the bottom of the shoals. It was nothing I would have thought twice about in a kayak, but paddling a loaded canoe is another thing. This sort of expedition paddling was new to me. I wasn't used to sitting upright above white water. I kept asking myself what could happen, and I always came up with the same answer. We might fill up and have to bail the boat, or worst-case scenario, we might flip and have to work the boat over to the shore through cold, early spring river water. We had all our gear tied in. It would ride with the boat, and there was little chance the eddy below would look like a yard sale.

"Oh, just keep it straight downstream and we can ride through about anything," V said when I told him I was nervous. "You want me to take it through by myself?"

The shoals below were just as Venable said it would be. We kept it straight and hit the big rolling waves in exactly the right place, one of a dozen smooth tongues of river water breaking the ledge into multiple glassy arcs. We worked down through several hundred yards of ledges with little waves and holes behind them.

After that little scrap of adventure we floated on down to the 99 Islands dam take-out three miles below on river left. I don't know exactly how many islands there actually are in the 99 Islands area, but there are quite a few. I imagine that before it was dammed the river there had an almost braided feel, a landscape Venable would have found familiar from the rivers in Alaska. We floated along. Then we heard gunshots.

A pistol, Venable said. "Nine-millimeter probably."

The shots were coming from the east bank. "Target practice?" I asked.

"That or somebody shooting at bottles in the river."

Then the shooter fired off about twelve rounds, paused, and a deeper report followed. "Now that's a semi-automatic assault rifle," Venable said.

"So that's what a fire fight would sound like?" I asked.

"Oh, I believe a fire fight would sound noisier than that."

An hour later, we saw the boat landing in the distance where we were meeting a friend who would take us back to Spartanburg. Just before landing we passed a great blue heron rookery on river right in a large tree along the edge of the impoundment. There maybe were ten birds with nests. Great blue herons are the large solitary waders you're most likely to see fishing on piedmont streams, and I don't often think of them congregating in rookeries. We floated slowly past this wild bloom of blue birds above us.

In many ways a rookery is the opposite of an abandoned textile mill like Cherokee Falls, a place where our economic culture played out in the past its notions of industry and profit, while often spoiling the land and water in the process. Those notions become obsolete locally, or too expensive, and the economic usefulness of a place moves on. Other forces take over—decay, rot, compost, nostalgia.

"Nature is nuance," the writer Edward Hoagland claims somewhere. I look up into the rookery tree and I see hope for the river and for us. The industry of herons is sustainable as long as the river itself is whole and healthy.

An old man, solitary as a heron, was fishing off the side of the boat dock when we arrived. He greeted us as we floated in, then he called off his little dog Ginger as we landed. His accent was old-growth piedmont mill town. He slurred his sentences until the vowels and consonants swam together in an audible gruel. Every sentence was slow as chilled molasses.

"Fishing any good?" I asked.

"Naaaaaw," he said.

"Well, it's a nice place to spend the day," I said.

"Day's right. You don't want to be here after night," he said. "Ginger, you get back over here. Them local boys will steal your tires. The game warden parked his truck, went out to do a little fishing. When he got back they'd sawed his lock and pushed that trailer right in the lake."

In the barely comprehensible local dialect leaking from under his cap, the old man told us that bad weather had moved through the South Carolina upcountry: "I'm telling you. They was hail stones big as golf balls, and they filled the back of my pickup ten inches deep."

He spit a clear stream in the dirt of something he'd been chewing all along. "You better be glad you weren't out in that pontoon," he said, nodding at our canoe. "It woulda tore y'all up."

Rivers, like the old fisherman or the herons that live along them, have complex histories. Cultures once clung to them. Towns and industries rose and disappeared on their banks. Now rivers are mostly occasional stages where weekend jubilees float through. Recreation has mostly replaced industry. Quiet has settled in the crooks and bends where mills once hummed and the workers once ached.

I'm still drawn to rivers, even though interstate highways often fulfill their original cultural niche ferrying our freight and dreams downstream. What I take away when I load my canoe and drive back to the suburbs is the lingering feeling that the world is bigger than us, and in motion. There are orders of history in South Carolina other than wars and industry, and one of the only ways to sense their presence is from the seat of a canoe. I float to feel the larger world. ☾

)

No Forever for Old Farms

There is something about an old farm that wants to be broken down. As time tests tin and weather wears wood, barns and outbuildings begin to lean and falter. Like old men teetering on canes, they rest feebly on stone foundations that hold them up despite the failure of everything else around them. They wobble in the wind, barely balanced on posts and pillars that keep them from falling flat on their facades. Their impending demise is hastened by loosening joints—mortise separating from tenon and nails falling out like rotting teeth. And yet, some old barns and sheds linger on. They were constructed not so much with neatly drawn plans to spec and scale, but rather with what was on hand. Aesthetic was never in the plan. Form was function. Were it not for something stronger than what we see, they would fail. The underpinning of stones, bricks, blocks, and mortar are the souls of the silos and sheds, and they stand for something durable—no matter the decaying timber they support.

Old farms sit in landscapes torn apart by toil and time. In their tenures, the dormers and doors of barns with roofs gabled and gambreled have been opened like eyes to see tons of soil turned to face the sun again and again. Sleeping with the chickens at dusk and waking with whippoorwills before the dawn, they have witnessed enough milk flowing from the swollen udders of cud-chewing cows to satisfy heaven's need for all the souls that ever could be saved. Crops—cotton, corn, tobacco, soybeans—were planted always to some promise and harvested with hope. And they've fallen like manna to the believers and failed with the faithless.

For those so disposed to gamble on the vagaries of soil and seed, heaven and hell have always been flip sides of the same coin. The echoes of bellowing bulls and murmuring sheep reverberate within the ancient pecan trees that still stand guard over what used to be. The old hickories, pocked by generations of obsessive-compulsive sapsuckers, still throw shade to the barnyards where the mule once stood awaiting gee or haw.

In the annual cycles, some measuring a century or more, old farms were warped in the back and forth between drenching rains and parching drought—wrenched apart nail by nail with each freeze and thaw. Disease in the form of decay was wrought by the jaws of millions of mites working day and night. When the wind blows, the timbers groan in the agony of an arthritic architecture that is living on borrowed time. The flapping scabs of rusted metal roofing hang on desperately, screaming to whatever will listen that they can still keep the elements at bay. All the while the barn owls, bats, and bees that have found refuge where none used to be know the truth. Cracks and gaps are holes now. Minor flaws have become major corruptions.

The buildings are not the only things that die. The skeletons of beasts of burden lie everywhere. Unceremoniously abandoned, the rusting, hulking frames of crippled tractors, disabled combines, and foundering trucks sit sinking into the ground, technological testaments to the fallibility of internal combustion. The things they dragged behind them—harrows, balers, sub-soilers, trailers—rest idly in a world of ravenous weeds and skulking white-throated sparrows, waiting for a plow horse of some kind to hitch themselves to.

Even the dirt dies. Soil that is no longer nurtured by plow or cow disintegrates in the sharp fingers of honey locusts, wild hedges of privet, and jungles of pokeweed. Buildings and implements die slow deaths and their memories linger like ghosts.

When one thinks of beautiful ruin, farms seldom come to mind. But patient travelers can find them along South Carolina's back roads. Thankfully there are places in the piedmont and upcountry that haven't been infected by the developer's disease. Get off the interstate and away from cell phone reception. Ride the fence lines and find the old farms. The fanciful names of Piedmont places—Plum Branch, Townville, Fair Play, Level Land—are not as important as the meandering that takes you to them.

I find a certain melancholic solace in the dying of an old farm. It is like the joy I find in gray, winter days. Cold, drab, and windy though they may be, I have a certain appreciation for the gravity they impart. It is okay to brood and think inwardly on sunless days. An old barn falling in on itself or a rusting silo drained of grain gives me permission to remember the melding of good and bad times. Moldering in that amalgamation of emotions is life to me, a type of Yin and Yang I suppose.

Yes, there is sadness to the senescence. Many families have bonded and some have flung apart in the struggle to make a living sweating into the soil. It's hard making sticky red clay or droughty sand yield something. Around the dinner table each night, prayers for the rain to stop or start, for the price per pound to drop or rise, are mercifully answered—and often brutally declined. With each request the children, having witnessed the struggle, decide, "Not me!" And so the farming families die like the buildings, slowly fragmenting until there is nothing left but the dysfunctional pieces and memories.

The connections between soil, sun, and sustenance were what held my family together for most of its existence. Our two hundred-acre farm near Edgefield, on the outskirts of a district called Colliers, was—still is—stuck in the middle of the Sumter National Forest, halfway between the "gypsy camp" (Murphy Village) and Old MacDonald's Fish Camp. Until recently, there wasn't even a road name to associate with the place—just a rural route and box number. It was a patchwork of forest and farm that my grandfather, Daddy Joe—a man I never knew—and then my father, James Hoover, harrowed, hoed, and harvested to sustain our family. Cows and crops kept the freezers full and helped my modestly paid schoolteacher parents keep their heads above water—mostly. Decisions about whether to buy hay or a few human groceries were sometimes in the balance.

My connections to that place are constantly reset by my senses—the sweet smell of hay stacked to the rafters, the sight of barn dust swirling in a shaft of fading sunlight like summer snow. I can still remember the first time I saw barn swallows nesting in a corner of the shed, twittering and fluttering as they raised their brood. Even back then, there were things that seemed ancient. There was so much left over from decades past that it felt more like a living museum than a working farm. There were old plow collars hanging on the wall and bits and pieces of disassembled plows and machines that never got put back together. I used to imagine what the sweaty horse looked like that wore that collar or what fantastic machine might reanimate itself from the heaps of scrap iron.

There was never a question of the place dying back then. Old and musty, it nevertheless thrived. Lizards and bobwhites were comforting signs that even in the decay, life continued.

Old farms are where weeds work to retake the world. The things kept at bay by mowing, cutting, and chemicals reemerge. There are the natives—broomsedge and ragweed—and the invaders too; multiflora rose, privet, and kudzu. Cedar trees stand like green-coated soldiers on sentry along sagging fence lines. Old orchards continue to bear fruit, but whitetails and other four-footed things pick the sweet harvests. In the winter, seeds and security create a thorny paradise for the sparrows. In the spring quail might find a home here too.

An old piedmont farm is no less magnificent to me than some ancient, faraway ruin where emperors lived lives of conquest and glory. In these piedmont places, the kings wore bib overalls and straw hat crowns. Wars were waged against weeds and weather, and there was little to gain except a few more bushels or pounds for the auction.

But, like my father, the most stoutly built barn will fall. The heart attack that killed him on a warm and greening day in April 1981 ended more than just his life. It killed the farm too. There was no one to put the work into the place to keep it from falling in.

Unlike his sudden death, the farm lingered for a while, laboring on life support but with the end never in doubt. And so almost thirty years after leaving, I return from time to time to see the remains. The built shells of what used to be sit largely in ruin. It didn't take long for gravity, weather, insects, and ne'er-do-wells to destroy things. The pole barn my father built to shelter hay and machines still stands, but I can barely see it for the loblolly pines and sweet gums that reclaimed the fields that once surrounded it. The adjoining hog pen that even in the best days seemed in disrepair is now covered in an impenetrable tangle of doghair pine, blackberry vines, and honeysuckle. The forest is slowly, surely, taking the land back.

Across the way, and a forest that used to be a pasture, my grandmother's house still stands. Alongside of it, the old log smokehouse does too.

The house has been ransacked and pilfered by trespassers picking through the lives of the people who used to live here. I expected as much, but I didn't expect the smokehouse to defy the decay. Probably built around the turn of the last century, it looked as if it had been entombed in a time capsule, with relics of share-cropping or even slavery lingering uncomfortably in its loosening logs.

The smokehouse was forbidden when I was a child, and I could only imagine its interior. I knew that meat used to be cured there and that it had become a storage place for all sorts of odd things. I remember it being dank, dark, and smelling of mold and fertilizer.

Lanham family farm smokehouse.
Photograph by J. Drew Lanham.

It was early March when I returned, between the remains of winter's cold and the teasing warmth that promised spring. My grandmother's daffodils and snowdrops were nodding yellow and white in the yard where she obsessively waged war against the weeds. I think those same weeds were simply the scouts of fate, harbingers of succession that would eventually take the place back one ecological step at a time towards old field and forest.

But the flowers had persisted, just like the smokehouse. All around it, things were falling in or growing up. Shrubs and trees were laying siege to what my ancestors had built, but somehow the log house, more than anything else, was bravely holding off the takeover. Even in all the falling down, something was still standing.

Old farms help me to remember what was. I can feel the struggles and triumphs that come with each season—spring's hope, summer's surge, fall's senescence and winter's dying. Whether it is my Home Place or someone else's, each time I linger in the shadow of a rusting silo or search for sparrows in the rank fencerow of an old pasture, I learn something about my own being and what will come. It is as sure as the leaves falling in October and birds flying south to warmer climes. Nature will have its inevitable way. Even as buildings are erected to last for generations—what some might call forever—I know that there is no such thing, especially for an old farm. ꒐

Photograph by Stan Lewis, courtesy of Caroliniana Library,
University of South Carolina, Columbia.

Birds, Fish, Water

"To heck with everybody and everything when birds are feeding and fish are biting. Stay late and lie like a dog if necessary."

From "Sometimes You Can't Find Them" by Havilah Babcock, originally published in *Outdoor Life* magazine. Babcock (1898–1964) was an outdoorsman, writer, and English professor at the University of South Carolina.

)

For the Birds

For three summers running in the 1960s, I spent two weeks at my aunt's home in Summerville. Daily trips to Folly Beach made my heart beat wildly. All that openness, sun, sea, and stretches of beach created a horizon like no other. I could see for miles.

When I went back home to eastern Georgia's forests and hills, the world closed in on me, and a longing for salt, sand, and spray consumed me. The surf kept calling in the whelk shell I held to my ear. Nothing's worse than growing up landlocked once you've had a taste of the sea.

Rural outposts grow big dreams in country boys and my dream was to live on the coast. Fate, however, had something else in mind—something *beyond* the coast—beautiful islands in a beautiful refuge called Cape Romain.

In 1978, I applied for a job as a scriptwriter and cinematographer for natural history films. Three finalists had to write a fifteen-minute script on the eastern brown pelican. My script, *The Magnificent Pelican,* cryptic wordplay involving my initials TMP, landed me the job, and for a deliciously brief time, I worked on the wild islands of Cape Romain Wildlife Refuge.

By Day

Even a sorry photographer knows the best light is at dawn. Up at 2 A.M., I would race the sun to the coast, the light falling in my wake on haunted, green swamps and oaks dripping with Spanish moss. The stars told me I was moving deeper into the land of blackwater rivers and white sands, so deep my journey would take me to the jumping-off place, a landing at McClellanville.

McClellanville, the quaint fishing village that welcomed Hugo ashore in 1989, sits just off Highway 17. Like a sea breeze, 17 blows through a land of tradition and awe. Where else do you see black women weaving sweetgrass baskets along green highway shoulders, come across a majestic name like Awendaw, or discover a wild refuge?

My first crossing was one to remember. In predawn darkness, we put out in a Boston Whaler manned by U.S. Fish & Wildlife Service boatman Herbert Manigault. The Whaler's engine hummed as we made our way through the estuary and breakwater to one of the last wild islands, Bulls Island. About three hundred yards from the marshy side, Herbert killed the engine. The unceasing sound of ten thousand Dewalt drills piercing steel crossed the water—mosquitoes by the millions.

I didn't care. I felt as if I were about to step onto the shores of Africa. And I felt this way for three summers in Cape Romain, a refuge that wraps barrier islands and salt marsh habitats around twenty-two miles of Atlantic coast. The refuge holds 35,267 acres of beach and sand dunes, salt marsh, maritime forests, tidal creeks, fresh and brackish water impoundments, and thirty-one thousand acres of open water. Nature rules. It is an ideal place to film wildlife for a simple reason: man has yet to ruin it.

Beautiful creatures and beautiful topography ennoble the refuge. Orange-billed oystercatchers and white egrets seem to vibrate against green spartina. Chocolate pluff mud that hints of sulfur counterbalances gritty beaches. Creeks are blue arteries that loop, double back, and nourish the green-gold spartina. The sea-ravaged maritime forest, however, leaves you breathless.

Every time I approached Bulls Island, D-Day came to mind. Rootballs of live oaks, loblolly pine, and cabbage palmetto litter the beach like the Czech hedgehogs and log ramps Germans planted on Omaha Beach. It looks like a battle scene, and the truth is it's a battle the trees lost.

The Atlantic's unrepentant tides undercut the trees' roots. Toppled trees, their sun-bleached limbs white as marble, lie strewn about, monuments to the moon and its tides. Stripped of foliage and bark and smoothed by sand and sea, the trees are about the end of things. Even death is beautiful in the islands.

We'd put ashore onto a wide low-slung panorama of sand, birds, noise, and heat. My mind made great leaps. A perfect overture, America's "A Horse With No Name" played in my head. Its lyrics of dry ground, "plants and birds," and a cloudless sky "full of sound" captured the rookery.

The birds of Cape Romain.
Photograph by Robert Clark.

And full of sound is right. Clamoring shorebirds swirl overhead, dropping bombs that necessitate wearing long sleeves and caps. (Never look straight up when you're in a rookery.)

The cup of life overflows here. The islands, pristine, sun splashed, and desolate, truly are for the birds because desolation is where the business of raising fledglings best takes place. In these Darwinian oases where survival of the fittest has long played out, I was an intruder, a spectator, a capturer of images.

Though sandpipers, plovers, oystercatchers, ruddy turnstones, laughing gulls, and scores of feathered species live here, my trips to Cape Romain involved pelicans, sand dunes, and sea turtles. They were the stars-in-waiting on a soundstage designed by nature.

Imagine clouds of birds flying over a mosaic of straw-stick nests filled with eggs and purple dollops.

That's what a pelican colony looks like. Amid this clamorous collage, I trained my Arriflex on fledgling pelicans, featherless, brownish-purple blobs. A rookery of jiggling fledglings is a dizzying thing and a bit unnerving. Many die and the sun-ripened smell overpowers you. But I liked the little rascals. I knew they were overcoming a hard time.

DDT's runoff from farm fields into rivers and then the sea put a hurt on the eastern brown pelican and other bird species. Plankton absorbed DDT, menhaden ate plankton, and pelicans ate menhaden in a game of food chain dominoes that weakened their eggs' calcium content. Thin and easily crushed, the flawed eggs put the pelican on the endangered species list in the early 1970s. DDT's ban and recovery efforts saved the pelicans. That was part of the story I was to tell.

Other birds played supporting roles. Least terns deserve at least a mention because they shared nesting space with the pelicans. A scrape in the sand just above the waterline—that's where least terns nest. Their eggs, tan with brown specks, look just like sand. They're near invisible. Not once did I crush an egg.

Today, least terns here and there colonize the graveled rooftops of buildings, commentary on how we've destroyed nesting habitat and another reason I love Cape Romain. Its feathery alchemy transforms sand scrapes into the seashore's grand aviary.

It was hot as Hell. There was no shade, just sun, sand, sky, and sea. The ancients believed the world consisted of fire, earth, air, and water. Their elements fit Cape Romain's islands. There the sun bears down on eggs destined to fill the sky in a great cycle of feathers, feeding, and seashore birdsong. And those sandy scrapes my feet avoided? They're remnants of ancient mountains, long washed into the Atlantic and heaped into isles.

Life's basics abound here. It's the perfect place for man not to build things. In all my time there, the tallest manmade structure on the island belonged to me: my tripod.

I was ocean-locked, an astounding turnaround from my youth, on a mission to tell the pelicans' story, but the birds never shared my delight. As stars are wont to do, they ignored me.

By Night

Sand dunes are more than mounds of sand. They're barriers to the sea and vital habitat to sea turtles and other species.

Filming nesting sea turtles demanded that we arrive late and stay late on the island, sometimes to three in the morning. We'd patrol the beach in a battered jeep—dropped there by a helicopter—looking for the telltale scrape marks that betrayed a female loggerhead turtle's crawl to the dune line.

One night we patrolled until 2:30 in the morning. No turtles. Herbert returned us to the landing in predawn darkness. As people slept on the mainland, we moved through the night unseen, like nighthawks. Faint light filled the sky, an accretion from Charleston and its suburbs. It seemed otherworldly.

On another trip, we were to put out for a night of turtle filming. It was late August and the nesting season would soon end. We were down to perhaps our final try. As we made our way into McClellanville, forks of lightning slashed the sky. We were advised not to head out. Common sense prevailed. We returned to Columbia.

The next day, breaking news. A family had been caught in the storms near McClellanville the evening before and lightning had struck their mast. The yacht had burned and the family had to abandon ship. We heard sharks ate them, something I never could confirm.

Our last chance came a week later. We hoped to find a turtle in the process of nesting, a sure thing. A turtle deep into nesting is, in a sense, paralyzed. She will not move once her eggs begin to fall—as poachers know all too well.

We set out around 9 P.M. beneath a full moon. Palmetto fronds splintered the moonshadowed ground into slivers of white, black, and silver. The marsh grasses and water shone silvery white. We patrolled a snow-white beach beneath luminous stars and a dazzling moon, a beautiful evening for luminaries such as nesting turtles.

We made two patrols. Nothing. Restless, we walked up and down the beach. Herbert, well aware this was our last dance, cautioned us. "She'll pause at the surf line and look around. She'll go back to sea if she spots you."

Close to midnight, we got out of the jeep again and walked north scanning the milky surf, which rushed in flirting with our feet before melting away. Nothing. For a long time the surf fell endlessly upon itself in a wavering line of gleaming water. Then a break, a concentrated area of darkness thirty yards up, interrupted the glowing foam.

A log had floated ashore. I nudged it with my foot and seafaring foxfire, pale green light like the aurora borealis, shimmered down the log's length. It's an image I'll never forget.

We kept patrolling. Around 2 A.M. we spotted a scrape running up to the dune line. Herbert circled behind the dune line to see how far along the nesting process might be. Soon he ran back, breathless, but with good news. She was on the nest. At last the elusive turtle egg-laying scene would go under the lights.

We walked up to a massive dune where a turtle was dropping slimy ping-pong ball-like eggs into a hole. This was no ordinary dune. It was *the* dune. A turtle comes back to lay eggs where she hatched. No one knows how they accomplish this miraculous navigation.

Covered with barnacles and shells, this turtle weighed about three hundred pounds. She smelled earthy, organic, hinting of salt and sulfur. Tears oozed from her eyes.

We watched her finish, cover the eggs with her flippers, dig another hole, and cover it to confuse the masked bandits of the night—raccoons. Then she crawled into the surf and disappeared beneath the dark, cresting Atlantic. Her babies would incubate in sun-warmed sand, nature's hatchery. Someday the few hatchlings that survived would return and begin the cycle anew.

Bye-Bye

I fell in love with the islands and their pelicans, sand dunes, and sea turtles. Cape Romain and its wild islands never failed to give me the feeling I was deep in the tropics. A sense of mystery and awe gripped me there and it never let go. It was a world I could only dream about as a boy. It was an adventure. It inspired me to write a novel. It was unpredictable and danger-ous. That flash of cobalt blue amid the sea oats—an indigo bunting? That slab of mud that just fell off the bank was not mud; it was a bull gator curi-ous to check me out.

I was last at Cape Romain in August 1983. Stepping into Herbert's Whaler for the last time, a wind ghosting over sun-struck salt marsh kissed me goodbye. I was about to change careers. I wouldn't be back.

A year later Don Henley's "Boys of Summer" hit the airwaves. Something about that song takes me back to Cape Romain every time I hear it. When I do, I see clouds of feathers, glistening sands, rippling marshes, nesting tur-tles, luminous logs, and beautiful desolation. "The summer's out of reach," Henley sang. Yes, out of reach. No more island hopping for me.

Now and then friends tell me they're going to Myrtle Beach. Their voices exude elation. "Can't wait to see the beach," they tell me. And off they go. The real beach, I know, is something they'll never see. They won't know, as I do, what the coast looked like in the beginning.

In 2007 I came tantalizingly close to Cape Romain. A friend and I drove down for an oyster roast at a farm overlooking an Awendaw estuary. It was a brisk Saturday early in March. Belted Galloway cattle dotted the pastures. The cows' saddle oxford hides of black and white had everyone's attention, everyone's except mine. I stared at the estuary. Somewhere out there were my islands, and March meant the pelicans would soon begin nesting.

For a few moments I was back. I stood there remembering my days and nights on the islands. I remembered crowning moments from my film years. My first bald eagle wheeling overhead. Spotting the rare swallow-tailed kite. Seeing a painted bunting clinging to a stalk of sea oats. Watching an osprey plunge into the estuary and emerge with a silvery fish in its talons.

I was back where dolphins run in and out of the estuary and loggerhead turtles crawl duneward to lay eggs. There in that sun-blasted, silver-moon islandscape, I captured images on film. There in that sea-level garden of sand, sea, and sun, I captured memories too as I tried to tell a story about a place that's truly for the birds, a place far from my Georgia home, a place beyond the coast. ☽

)

Holy Ground

Burrells Ford is for me a little like Bethel was for Jacob. He stopped to camp for the night. Choosing a rock that looked a little like a pillow, he made himself as comfortable as he could. He had a dream of angels ascending and descending a ladder reaching to heaven. Maybe the ladder was spiraled like the double helix of his DNA. He was, after all, sleeping in a place where his grandfather Abraham had worshiped. When Jacob awoke, the dream was vividly etched in his mind. "Surely the Lord is in this place and I was not aware of it," he thought to himself.

At Burrells Ford I have slept on rocks, but I have never dreamed of a ladder. Still, it's holy ground for me. When you walk beside a mountain stream, the wind in your face, sun glistening on a waterfall, you may sense the presence of God. The laurels in bloom in the spring, a summer thunderstorm moving up the gorge, the bright colors of fall—these are all evidence of a divine hand.

So when I heard a call, so to speak, I knew how to respond. "Dr. Kirk, will you take me trout fishing?" The question came from Luke, a young man who had been a high school classmate of our children. He and his parents are friends of our family.

Now, as a Ph.D. candidate at Cornell, Luke wanted to experience one of the things he had missed. He had never angled for trout, so I promised a trip when he was back home. Our opportunity came the following Christmas. There was only one place to go for his first mountain fishing trip, and that was my favorite trout fishing spot—Burrells Ford on the Chattooga River.

Under the shadow of Whiteside Mountain, the highest sheer cliffs in the Blue Ridge Mountains, the Chattooga River headwaters spill over small ledges and waterfalls. The mountain stream enters a narrow and treacherous

The author at Burrells Ford.
Photograph by Betsy Neely.

gorge. Gathering momentum with sharp drops in elevation, the river follows a twisting route over continuous rapids and around massive boulders.

The Chattooga is one of the few remaining free-flowing mountain streams in the Southeast. Dense forests characterize the primitive area. In 1974 Congress designated the Chattooga a Wild and Scenic River.

In 1811, Andrew Ellicott, a surveyor, settled a boundary dispute between Georgia and North Carolina. He marked a large rock in the Chattooga River. Ellicott Rock is the point where the boundary lines of South Carolina, North Carolina, and Georgia join.

As the river leaves the gorge it flattens, flowing wide and smooth between Georgia and South Carolina. At a shallow place, an old rutted road crossed the rocky bed of the river, allowing wagons drawn by oxen, mules, or draft horses to travel across the state line. The crossing is called Burrells Ford.

I love this area of northwestern South Carolina. It was here, in the early spring of 1985, where I landed my largest rainbow trout, a nineteen-inch male sporting the distinctive hooked jaw or kype.

I am sure the fish had been a breeder released in the fall from the fish hatchery upstream.

It was here where I had previously experienced a dramatic confrontation with a large black snake. The serpent swam from the Georgia side across the swift current to the place I was fishing on the South Carolina bank. I doubt that snake had ever before encountered a human. He was completely unafraid of me. He gave me quite a pause and a sharp bloody bite on the thumb.

Before the Chattooga was declared a Wild and Scenic River, campers could drive down a side road all the way to Burrells Ford Campground. Now, though, a protective corridor has been established, cutting off all direct motorized access. The short hike may deter some tent campers, but there will never be a recreational vehicle at Burrells Ford.

Most camp sites are beneath the shady canopy of hardwood and hemlock trees, but some sites are in glades near the river. I have pitched a tent here numerous times. I prefer to be within earshot of the whitewater. Exhilarating—that's how I describe sleeping beside a mountain stream and waking up in fresh mountain air.

Even in late December, Burrells Ford and the Chattooga were where I wanted to take my friend Luke. On Friday morning we drove west on S.C. Highway 11 through the area known as the Dark Corner of South Carolina. Turning up S.C. Highway 130, we ascended the Blue Ridge escarpment, stopping at a lookout above Jocassee Gorges. Mountain streams feed beautiful Lake Jocassee, the best-kept secret in South Carolina. The water is deep and clear, so clear that in water twenty feet deep, I could see a largemouth bass pick up the plastic worm on the end of my fishing line.

Then we drove just across the state line into North Carolina. A short walk from a parking area took us to another overlook and a spectacular view of Whitewater Falls.

We made our way back down N.C. Highway 107 to the Walhalla State Fish Hatchery. Nothing whets a fisherman's appetite more than seeing concrete tanks teeming with rainbow trout, the very fish that will eventually stock the streams and rivers of the Upstate. "This is the first time I have seen rainbow trout," my young friend said, gazing at the vats filled with fish.

Several miles down a dusty gravel road, we crossed over the Chattooga River on the Burrells Ford Bridge, which marks the border between Sumter National Forest in South Carolina and Chattahoochee National Forest in Georgia. This section of the whitewater stream has almost always been a spot where I could be sure to catch a trout. Luke and I fished for hours, changing locations several times. We caught nothing.

We did see a belted kingfisher swoop down, plucking a fish from the water. In retrospect, it was the catch of the day.

After lunch, sitting on the tailgate of the truck, I suggested we go up King Creek. Sometimes I've caught trout there when I couldn't catch them in the big river.

Luke and I walked down the Forest Service road toward the campground, then up a mountain trail, about two miles, following King Creek. We paused at likely spots where we might hook a trout. Even on a warm day in December, the only bites we had were from mosquitoes. We did not catch anything.

At one sunny spot, I heard rustling in the dry leaves. I was almost sure it was a rattlesnake. Three times I heard the distinctive rattling sound. I held still, searching the sides of the trail with my eyes, but I never saw the source of the noise.

Giving whatever it was a wide berth, we continued up the trail to King Creek Falls, a stunning waterfall about seventy feet high. We sat on a log watching water spill from the top of the mountain into a pool below. Perhaps it is the backward slant of the rocks, but the drop appears to be higher. Sometime in the past a massive tree fell from the top of the cascade, stabbing its top into the basin at the foot of the waterfall. As long as I have been visiting the place, the huge log has remained unmoved.

We made our way back down the creek, returning to the river. We heard a loud splash. My friend asked if it was a squirrel. "Nope, too big a splash for a squirrel; too small for a bear," I replied. "I don't know."

A fuzzy head bobbed up in the water. Luke blurted, "It might be a muskrat!"

It disappeared quickly. I knew it would pop up downstream. Sure enough, the head resurfaced, this time with a companion. Not muskrats, but river otters, frolicking as river otters are wont to do.

"It's a good thing we don't have any fish to carry," I observed on our hike up the mountain back to the truck.

A man walking up the Forest Service road passed us, carrying a small ice chest.

I asked him, "How was the fishing?"

"Didn't catch enough to keep," he said, his euphemism for "didn't catch anything."

Others coming down the trail inquired, "How's the fishing?"

"Didn't catch enough to keep," I answered. A good line, I thought, so I made it my own.

For supper we enjoyed fried salt-and-pepper catfish and hushpuppies at a local fish camp.

The fishing is usually good in this favorite haunt of mine, so pristine with its meeting of mountains and waters. There is hardly anything better than trout, fresh from the river, cooked over a campfire.

The truth is that when I visit Burrells Ford, fishing is incidental. I come here for something more essential than a trout supper. I hope my friend Luke experienced something similar.

In my life, I am prone to major or minor things and miss the more important experiences. Focused on my busy schedule, I lose sight of the big picture. I am apt to think that when I finally collapse in bed at night from sheer exhaustion I will achieve peaceful rest. I am likely to think my frantic attempts to meet my many responsibilities are somehow holding the universe together. At Burrells Ford I find a needed realignment of my perspective, a resetting of priorities.

A visit to this holy ground gives my panting spirit a chance to catch up with my racing mind and my weary body. At Burrells Ford, I can't help but paraphrase Psalm 23. He makes me lie down in a green forest, He leads me beside whitewaters, and my soul is restored. ☽

Photograph by David Soliday, courtesy of Robert Marvin/Howell
Beach & Associates, Inc.

The Comforts of Home

"This is the area I understand and these are the people I love."

Internationally known landscape architect Robert Marvin
(1920–2001), on why he chose to stay in Walterboro

My Quarter Acre of Paradise

Our house sits on a four-acre plot of land bequeathed to my wife by her father who owned land handed down for generations. This land is on SC Highway 27 in Dorchester County between Ridgeville and Givhans. In 1976 we cut our lot off from an eleven-acre plot that was part of twenty-two acres that my father-in-law owned with his brother. Feed corn had been planted here season upon season to feed his livestock. We still lived out of state at that time and acquiring the land was part of our grand retirement plan to move back to South Carolina and build a house, a fish pond and a vegetable garden. When I retired in 1989 our house was livable but not fully completed, so we moved in and continue to work on it. A hundred feet behind the house we planted a small vegetable garden of tomatoes, cucumbers, peppers and greens. This is when I discovered the serenity of gardening and began to develop a deep gratitude for the quarter acre of space behind our house. Countless other feelings were yet to become clear.

Vegetable gardening has been a part of human life since ancient times. There are records from the earliest cultures describing the importance of the family garden. Through the centuries, growing foodstuffs in small and large quantities has been largely responsible for the survival of the species. It is so important and profitable an undertaking that it is now mainly controlled by corporations with their own scientists who can modify seeds, cultivate hybrids, and improve chemical pesticides. Besides size, tranquility is the main distinction between family gardening and commercial farming. In family gardening there is also the possibility of raising a higher-quality crop free from genetic modifications.

When I laid out the half-acre for our vegetable garden none of this was on my mind; rather, I thought of having read Henry David Thoreau while

I was in college. *Walden* is Thoreau's account of his self-reliant vegetable garden and his life at Walden Pond. Thoreau removed himself from what was modern life in 1845 Concord, Massachusetts, and moved a mile in the woods around Walden Pond where he built a small house. He wanted to experience nature, prove his self-reliance, and contemplate the essentials of life. Thoreau developed such a high degree of serenity in the two years he lived alone in the woods that he wrote his timeless book *Walden; or, Life in the Woods.* He also had abundant time to contemplate the civil society of his time. Thoreau had been jailed once for resisting paying his poll taxes as a protest of slavery and the Mexican-American War. His examination of those events through the prism of nineteenth-century government control over the citizenry produced his essay "On the Duty of Civil Disobedience," which later helped to free nearly a billion people in India and twenty-five million Africans in America. Mohandas Gandhi modeled his strategy of nonviolent civil disobedience against British colonization after Thoreau's theory of civil disobedience and in 1949 freed his people from British rule. Martin Luther King, Jr., studied both Thoreau and Gandhi and modeled his nonviolent civil rights campaign from what he learned about human nature from these two men and shamed America into a more civil relationship with its black population. The time Henry David Thoreau spent in his garden on Walden Pond and the seeds he sowed in "On the Duty of Civil Disobedience" produced a legacy that changed the world.

I started my garden as an expansion of the 6 x 2 x 2-foot wooden box I grew tomatoes and collard greens in on the terrace of the sixteenth floor of the high-rise building in New York City where I lived. Few tools were needed for my mini urban garden. When I started my quarter-acre garden I had no equipment of my own. I borrowed a tiller and hoes for my first two seasons. The store where I purchased seeds also sold young ducks, which gave me the idea to divide the quarter-acre in half and have a pond dug. I soon found someone to dig the pond for me at a price that was reasonable. I stocked the pond with fish and brought ducks to live in and around it. This quarter-acre began shaping up to hold my admiration and attention, and it became hard to leave it for dinner and bed.

By my third season I bought my own tiller and hoes and other gardening tools. I fenced in the whole area and separated the pond from the garden with fencing to prevent the ducks from getting into the garden and damaging young crops. This also helped keep deer out, but not completely—what gardener does not have a deer problem?

Horace Mungin and his grandson, Nazareth Mungin, at work in Paradise.
Photograph by Gussie Mungin.

My garden is 150 feet wide with sixty-foot rows. My wife and I made our planting hills by pulling dirt to the mound with hoes. We were able to get fifty rows out of the space. This is hard work, but we love it. Starting from the left I planted six rows of white corn, four rows of butterbeans, four rows of Blue Lake string beans, two rows of flat string beans, four rows of field peas, four rows of peanuts, two rows of tomatoes, two rows of peppers, one row of squash, one row of zucchini, one row of eggplants, two rows of onions, one row of scallions, two rows of collard greens, one row of mustard greens, two rows of okra, four rows of cucumbers, four rows of watermelons, one row of lettuce and two rows of white potatoes.

I also planted sunflower seeds randomly around the garden as an ornamental beautifier.

Anticipating these vegetables growing from the ground was almost as exhilarating as actually seeing them rise up in their different forms and color shades. In the evenings I found it hard to tear myself away from them. This was quickly becoming my most favorite spot on earth. Sometimes in the evenings sitting out by the garden with a cold drink, I would swear I could see the crops grow. Every year since then we have planted some rotating mix of these same crops.

Not every planting season produces the same results. There are so many factors that have to come together just right for a good harvest. Some of these factors, like soil condition, planting at appropriate times and plant maintenance are under my control. But others, like rain, drought, and seed quality, are not. So there are times when I'm disappointed with my quarter acre of paradise. But it's the ability to cope with whatever comes in my garden that fortifies me to handle the disappointments that come in my larger life.

Immediately after we started to have a relatively large enough harvest, my wife learned to can fruits and vegetables. She also mastered a quick-freeze method that she uses on vegetables to retain their freshness. There is a time during the harvest that our operation is split between the garden and the kitchen and even the computer room where I make labels for the jars. By September we have jars of canned tomatoes, string beans, tomato and okra mixed; plus peaches, pears, and figs from our fruit trees. We store the vegetables we consume during the winter in the freezer in the laundry room—mostly butterbeans, field peas, okra, and sweet white corn. The sense of self-sufficiency this provides is reassuring. It is good to know we can feed ourselves if the food chain ever breaks down—a possibility so real that the Bill and Melinda Gates Foundation, along with a host of other major organizations, established a "doomsday seed bank" in a desolate mountain near the North Pole to store copies of every seed known to man.

My quarter acre of paradise has aesthetic attractions only lovers of agricultural nature can appreciate. When the crops are midway through the season and most of them are developing produce is when I am most keenly aware of how much I love this spot. And to see the wondrous faces of the sunflower plants hovering over the crops is a pure delight.

My work in the garden offers me a solitude that dissipates the complex clutter of modern living from my head—life in the garden is reduced down to the simple essentials. This sublimation increases my capacity to think clearly on other matters, particularly whatever writing project I am working on at the time. Often I walk a few steps back to the pond and watch the ducks frolic in the water and wonder where they sleep at night. Or I walk the length of the garden, surveying the progress of the crops. And I remember Thoreau's transcendental notion, which is clear to me nearly a half-century after my years in college: "Heaven is below our feet as well as above our heads." ☽

A Little Different, a Little the Same

North Augusta. Doesn't even have its own name. North of someplace else. Most cities spread to the west and the north. Why? Sun? Prevailing winds? Maybe something city fathers read in a book.

Augusta (Georgia) couldn't spread north because of the Savannah River; and even if they could've swum that, another state, South Carolina, rose on the other side. So North Augusta grew up using all the advantages of Augusta without having to endure any of its disadvantages—traffic, crowds, politics, garbage collection, garbage disposal, garbage period, crime.

North Augusta was never a bedroom community. It was itself, from the beginning, looking down on the big town the way little towns always look down on big towns. Sixty million years ago, or thereabouts, Augusta was the bottom of the ocean. North Augusta, and Summerville, where affluent Augusta lived, were the shores, the beaches, the sand hills.

So North Augusta grew up without a main street. James U. Jackson, who founded the town, saw it as an Athens, a Greek city climbing a hill. He managed six columned mansions; four still exist. One burned, another was "architected," and then demolished for a church. Columns—we pronounce it "kol-yums." So as not to confuse it with the writing in a newspaper.

We walked to school, two old brick buildings at the bottom of the hill. The teachers remembered the War-ugh, cried when we sang "Tenting To-night" and "Maryland, My Maryland," to the tune, though we didn't know it, of "Tannenbaum, O Tannenbaum."

Recess, I clung to the side of the building, desperately trying to hold up a hateful pair of scratchy, too-big wool under drawers my cousins who lived next door had willed me when they outgrew them. "Save you from catching cold," my mom said. Never mind it was May.

Seven Gables (1903–2008).
Art by Henry Wynn.

My cousins! Their father, Edison Marshall, was a—yes!—successful writer. He had been stationed in Augusta during World War I, married Daddy's sister, and settled into Palmetto Lodge, a huge, never-meant-to-be-lived-in adjunct to Hampton Terrace, the largest wooden hotel in America that burned, not a single lost life, New Year's Eve, 1916. The lodge, a gabled Tudor stack my uncle grandly rechristened "Seven Gables," though it had eight, had operated as a sort of clubhouse for card playing (gambling?), socializing, shooting (outside—clay pigeons), and snacking (drinking). A place for the hotel guests to eat up their time between meals back at the hotel dining room.

Seven Gables had a million rooms, front stairs, back stairs, an attic, cellars, balconies, dark passages that seemed to lead nowhere, a gun room, a two-story front hall, infinite places to get into trouble and hide, jump out and scare any of the people who worked in the house. Black, white, I don't think we knew the difference. They did, though, and viewed us as part of the annoyances connected with cooking and cleaning. There were dark red drinking glasses for the help. Our glasses, probably like our consciences at the time, were crystal clear.

The house was decorated with dead animals, water buffalo heads, seladangs, elephant tusks, and feet—hollowed out and lidded as humidors for cigars and paper clips and such—tiger and leopard rugs, grizzly bear throws. A huge barracuda trophy over the door into the dining room, its mouth menacingly open, got us into trouble when we climbed up on a stepladder and put an apple into its teeth Christmas Eve. We children couldn't wait to grow up, have our own rifles and hang dead heads on the walls in our rooms.

A Little Different, a Little the Same 191

We—my brother, my parents—lived next door to the big house. A wide lawn separated the big house from the little house. There was a barn at the back of the lot. My uncle thought we shouldn't be afraid of anything, ordered snakes from a herpetarium in Florida, showed us how snakes could swallow other creatures bigger than their jaws. Gleefully we tossed mice and bunnies into the cage, a wire cage too close to our house for comfort, and watched with fascination as the devoured animal, shape still visible through the snake's scaly skin, passed down the length of the reptile's body.

My aunt and my mom would pay my brother and me a penny per blossom to climb up the big magnolia trees and pick off the dead brown blooms before they had the garden club meeting. My mother would stand out on the ground below, directing us like a fighter pilot in World War II movies. "Bad one at two o'clock high!" "Left, way left, quarter to three." This ended when my brother, stretching out to the limits of his young limbs, fell and broke his arm. The garden club meeting went on without apology, the ladies sitting out in lawn chairs, their eyes fastened, I imagined, on the two or three dark blossoms we hadn't managed to reach.

All this ended with the war. My uncle for some odd reason thought they were going to bomb North Augusta. "We have the best drinking water in the world," he said. "From the river." "And there's the fort, Camp Gordon. And who can explain what the Japanese and the Germans are thinking?"

They moved to Florida. And then to Cuba. My older cousin had been drafted. They wanted to be near him. He must've loved boot camp with his parents and sister hovering nearby.

I missed my cousins so much my parents who could ill afford it, not to mention the difficulty of getting a train ticket, somehow sent me age six, to Miami. I still remember the soldiers on the train, going off to flight school and maybe their deaths later, laughing at me, sneaking me swallows of beer.

North Augusta became a different place. No gasoline, no tires, no shoe leather, no sugar; we had to stay where we were.

Katherine and Tip Mealing, two sister schoolteachers—the Mealings were an old North Augusta family, their brother a doctor, a wonderful doctor, hybridized camellias and lived in Look Away Hall—ran a little swimming pond, Getzens. The pond had had exhibitions of aquatic feats and displays in the days of the old hotel, days when northern visitors felt they owned—and probably did—the south. Katherine taught us how to do the frog kick, the Australian crawl, how to rescue a drowning person, how to stay under water for what seemed like a week. Everybody went swimming at the pond. It was a family place—a description she being single, her sister, too, would've despised. We watched the newspapers for photographs of the older boys who'd been her lifeguards and were now overseas in the war, photographs of their heroism and sadly, twice, their deaths.

Katherine and Tip taught in Augusta and would drive their nephew, Buddy, now a doctor like his dad, and my brother and me to the old Academy where we wore uniforms, uniforms left over from the war when it ended, so called "tropical wool" creations that still reeked, no matter how many times sponged or dry-cleaned, of death in the Coral Sea. The wool— could anything more hatefully bring back the memory of the wool underwear my cousins had draped on me?—still scratched and itched.

North Augusta changed, became Republican, purposeful with the Bomb Plant. Men, and women with engineering degrees inhabited the town, caused suburbs to be built. Hammond Hills, once Indian Mound, was where we as Boy Scouts had dug for arrowheads from the famous Allendale chert quarries, where those first humans had found the stone for sharpening.

The town needed more schools, more teachers. Oddly, it was discovered some of the northern engineers' boys could play football. So locals forgot, forgave.

The town somehow maintained its village appearance, village mentality. Nobody bothered it—it was still another state to Augusta realtors and developers. North Augusta had stores and doctors, an undertaker, and whatever else you needed daily, but you still drove to Augusta—new malls—or Columbia, or with the highways, Atlanta, for big purchases, things that had to go in trucks, things that required a certain space and style.

Gradually North and South, something that hadn't happened right after the War-ugh, blended. North Augusta natives and Savannah River Siters opened up to each other.

And suddenly, or slowly, North Augusta became a place to be. It had never been, to Augusta, the "wrong" side of the tracks, simply the other side. My friends in high school in Augusta jokingly inquired whether they had to have a passport to go over there.

Clean, safe schools good enough to send your children to, lower taxes, closer to Augusta—hospitals, the military, some jobs—than Augusta was to Augusta, and closer to the mountains, the beach, and cheap liquor, North Augusta simply became, North Augusta. Who could argue with that?

Ed Rice, a painter whose studio is down the street, said the mayor stopped at his house lately, told Ed that Ed usually left the left front door of his truck open when he was hauling out canvas and so forth, but that this morning his right front door was open. Was anything wrong, the mayor wanted to know. I called down to the city hall to complain about my water bill—I had a leak and didn't know it—the mayor answered the phone, said, "Is that you, Starkey?"

Seven Gables burned to the ground summer before last and with it half my childhood. My cousin's son inherited the tiger skin, was in the Navy, tried to take the tiger skin on board his ship. "No, no, son," said the captain. "We take women, have to, the government, used to be considered bad luck, women, but we draw the line at striped kitties."

One summer, how many years ago, the woods that Katherine and Tip and the Mealings owned caught fire. Everybody was summoned. We cut trenches, hauled buckets, tossed sand, and miraculously, aided by a soft summer rain, put out the fire, saved the woods. Katherine and Tip gave every one of us a season pass to the pond. Its face value was two dollars and fifty cents, but its heart value was a million dollars. We proudly put it in our first wallets, skimpy cloth folds into which our parents had inserted a dollar bill—"you are never, I mean never, to spend this. This is in case something happens. So you can get home, or to the hospital, wherever you need to go, and people will know you're not just somebody else." My friends and I had our season pass inside our "wallets" and insisted on showing it to Tip at the gate each time we went swimming, though she told us she knew who we were, knew we had season passes.

North Augusta has changed less than most towns in the CSRA—initials for Central Savannah River Area—a name devised by a TV station ad campaign. Lack of change may be a good thing, like a gated community without a gate, or a gate that has a clock above it, a clock whose hands are standing still. Katherine and Tip's woods are malls now. Their house has disappeared in the few woods that are left. Getzens Pond feeds the water hazard on the golf course down by the river, the flood plain the new dam at Clark Hill has made safe. They say. We have a new city hall, a K-Mart, a Walmart, a new library. North Augusta seems to have everything every other town has, but it's still unlike every other town.

Last summer my lawn mower was stolen. Thirty minutes after I reported it, the N.A. police found it, brought it back. They laughed—well, smiled when I said I wouldn't have minded if the culprits had planned to mow some grass in the neighborhood. Like my front yard. Efficient law enforcement. And a sense of humor. ☽

Home

I'm an Army Brat.

I often joke that I've lived in seventeen states, but not one of them was a state of despair. Most of my youth was spent out West, in what seemed like movie settings where horses were— thrillingly—still a regular part of life. After three years in Hawaii I can attest that state is the paradise it is portrayed to be, with balmy weather, relaxed attitudes and a sense of bliss that seemed to be wafted in by the soft, tropical trade winds. During high school, I had free rein to roam the Georgetown area of Washington, D.C., to hear the amazing rock and blues bands that city attracted. When I think of those places, I get pangs of what I once thought was "homesickness," although I never really had a feeling of home.

By the time Dad retired, after twenty-five or so houses I'd lived in, the only vaguely true sense of home I'd ever felt was at my grandparents' house in North Carolina. I got to live there for a year at age twelve while my Dad was overseas and my mother settled her parents' estate. I soaked up Mother's stories and vicariously felt her sense of home, and I got a picture of how warm and secure it must have been for her to have grown up in the same house all her life.

My heartstrings tugged at me for many years about that house, with the occasional fantasy about buying it and making it my "forever home," as is said about rescued pets, perhaps with the hope of taking the stray out of me.

Our family had never lived in South Carolina, so I happened upon South Carolina in a whimsical way. After graduating from high school in the D.C. area and "serving" a year at a convent—I mean college that my conservative father picked for me in North Carolina, my parents decided to retire in Columbia because of the weather, the nearby military post, and the University of South Carolina. As a good daughter should, I came down to help them get settled, but with absolutely no intentions of staying. My plans were to throw a few boxes in the house, give them lots of hugs and kisses, then skitter off to cooler climes (literally and figuratively).

Those plans changed in quick succession because I located a cute guy, a stray German shepherd, and a starving Tennessee Walking Horse in Columbia—all of whom I felt needed my rescue skills. I had responsibilities to that trio, so I decided it was in everyone's best interest if I stayed on temporarily—ahem—in Columbia.

The cute guy attended USC. Because I was looking for a new college, I enrolled there too. The original campus, the Horseshoe, was breathtaking in its beauty and Ryder (the dog) went everywhere with me. He sat patiently beside my desk as I attended each class. He majored in squirrels and was graduated Summa Cum Rodentia with a minor in dog psychology. Other collegian hipsters of the era began to bring their dogs, but were told it was a no-go by the professors. Fortunately for us, Ryder was allowed to stay and in fact was given a certificate of graduation—with honors! I believe he is the only dog who ever graduated from USC. (Though I refused to participate in graduation exercises, one of my psychology professors gave Ryder his "college dog-gree" papers.)

I worked my way through college training horses and bartending at several establishments. So for a long time the Five Points area of Columbia was central to my world and I heard live music almost every night of the week. Five Points became my site for nightlife because of the constant flow of musical acts passing through its venues. The various clubs and bars that have hosted live music through the years are legendary. Oliver's Pub, The Coal Company, Greenstreets, Rockafellas, The Elbow Room, Group Therapy and many more have promoted unknown bands that have gone on to reach the top of the charts.

An opportunity arose to move to California shortly after I graduated. I took a long visit there, working on a place to stay, and found employment. After six weeks, it became clear that although I could afford to ship Ryder across the country, I would have to sell my beloved horse, Joker, to make the move. Heartstrings, or heart-reins, were tugged so hard that I returned.

A few years later, I took a job at the university. My office was on the Horseshoe, providing me with an 1801 window through which to view its beautiful vistas. I lived nearby. I found it humorous that it took me longer to walk from my parking spot through the Horseshoe to work than it did

One small part of the USC Horseshoe.
Photograph by Tracy Fredrychowski.

to drive from home to the parking spot, but I was always inspired by those daily walks past the grand magnolias and monuments on campus.

In Ryder's honor, I befriended the squirrels on the Horseshoe. One in particular had a nub for a tail, so I nicknamed him Chip. For a period of what I'm guessing is a squirrel's lifetime, Chip met a colleague and me at the edge of the Horseshoe each morning and walked us to work. Then I suppose he would spend the day going about his squirrel obligations. He faithfully returned each evening to walk us back across the 'Shoe. I still have no idea why that animal friendship began or ended, but I wonder if perhaps Ryder came back as a Horseshoe squirrel.

While working and attending graduate school at USC, I was asked to host a radio show at the university's award-winning radio station, WUSC-90.5 FM. After much initial shyness and balking, the station manager persuaded me to share my love of music with the community. The "Blues Moon with Clair DeLune" radio show was launched rather shakily in the midsummer of 1990. Decades later, the show is going strong despite my intermittent predilection for dead air. I am honored to have been at 90.5 (the station) since '90.5 (the year).

The connection between the live music scene in Five Points and the radio show kept me rocking and rolling from one great show to the next for many years. But sometimes, as my military father would attest, duty calls. Changes in my professional life provided the opportunity to take a directorship position at a college in North Carolina, where I still had many friends and family. The offer came with increased responsibilities, a great title, and a big jump in pay.

When consulted about the decision to move "Nawth," some friends in Columbia extolled the virtues of North Carolina versus the drawbacks of South Carolina—as if the former were heaven compared to the latter's hell. I am of the opinion that any place is what you make of it, so that didn't sway me, but the professional opportunity did. Frankly, I thought the move would be less like "leaving home" and more like "going home."

I was excited.

I was also wrong.

North Carolina is nice. I do love it there. The job was good. The people were great! I worked hard. I stayed with a fabulous friend and postponed a commitment to buy a house for a year, following my dad's wise counsel.

But South Carolina called to me. Upon visits back, as I drove past the Horseshoe and through Five Points, I felt a pang of familiarity that was wholly unfamiliar to me. It felt particularly peculiar one Friday night as I drove into the heart of Five Points on Harden Street. Without knowing why, I stopped the car. I got out and smelled the air. I watched the traffic light change more than once at Harden and Greene streets. I drank in the feeling of Five Points and Columbia.

I wept.

I determined what the feeling was. I was homesick for the first time in my life.

I desperately wanted to come home.

And I knew I had a home *here:* in Columbia. I had a home among the tree-lined streets of the Shandon neighborhood and along the University of South Carolina pathways. Under the copper dome of the statehouse and in the little shopping village of Five Points.

I still lived and worked in North Carolina. But, Columbia was calling me, and this time I listened.

One particular series of actual calls came with a job offer. A job I applied for years before had been unfrozen and they wanted me, but I had previously turned them down. In a wonderful twist of fortune, they called to ask one last time. It was then I realized I not only wanted to move home to be closer to my dad and friends here, but I had a way to come home—really home—in fact, to the first real feeling of home I'd ever felt.

That feeling of home has stayed with me ever since. When I drive through Five Points or past the campus after a trip somewhere, no matter how pretty or wonderful or exciting that place was, I revel in the fact that I live in beautiful Columbia, South Carolina—with all its wonderful places and people.

It's funny that two stray animals led me to finding my way home. ☽

)

Tobacco Roads

The place I love most is no place in particular but every field and small town in South Carolina's historic yet unprosperous Pee Dee. More specifically, I love hundreds of miles of asphalt in Florence, Georgetown, Horry, Marion and Williamsburg counties. Not exactly the tourism center of the universe, thank God, but an essential place where the aroma of rain-drenched grass and flat, loamy earth are punctuated by Coca-Cola colored rivers and scenic tobacco fields rich with memories.

Memories of jumping as a four-year-old from stack to stack of tobacco at auction in the early August heat. Of kitchen aromas, including essences of fried chicken, collard greens and biscuits swirling throughout my grandmother's house on Main Street in Hemingway. Memories of standing around the barbecue pit at Mr. Okie Baxley's house near Stuckey every Friday night while the stars shot from the smoky sky. Mr. Okie and Daddy discussed whose crops and high school football teams were season-ready.

My mama always said she was afraid the only way she'd escape the Pee Dee was in a pine box, but she dragged my father kicking and screaming to Columbia when they retired in 1983, to be near my autistic brother and immerse herself in the politics. Meanwhile, I was in Columbia, gyrating in the political milieu myself, within walking distance of my parents and my mother's precious sister, Aunt Eleanor, and longing deeply for a way back home.

Then a college friend called one day to tell me he was leaving his job in Conway and asked if I wanted it. The call came one Thursday night when the man I'd secretly vowed to marry was at the door. I was poised to shag the night away, measuring my ring finger for the right size. But, he didn't want a commitment, at least not to me.

Horry County barn.
Photograph by Jack Thompson.

So, the next day, Friday, I called my friend and begged for that promised job.

"Fast turnaround," my friend said.

"We broke up. I'm ready to move."

"Send your resume and hurry," he said. "The search closes Monday."

This was before the days of e-mail or even fax machines, when the U.S. Postal Service was my only prayer.

Surely enough my resume arrived on Monday, I received the call for an interview on Tuesday, resigned from my Columbia job on Wednesday and started the new one the next Monday morning. For a moment Mama took it personally. She had just moved nearby and here I was yanking up my new roots to go home.

"It's not personal," I said. "I simply love the Pee Dee."

In 1984 Horry County, then part of the old Sixth Congressional District, was as rural as Florence or Marion—maybe not quite so rural as Williamsburg. But Williamsburg was only an hour away. Close enough to climb in my silver-and-red velour Monte Carlo—yes, it fairly encapsulated the essence of a brothel—and roam a complex web of secondary roads, all four pimpmobile windows open wide. I celebrated sunrises on Black River and sunsets along Murrells Inlet. Ate quail and drank dark liquor. Signed on for golf lessons and hacked up every manicured golf course on the Barbecue Trail. Sneezed frenetically over every freshly turned field. Ate breakfast at greasy spoons from Kingstree to Marion; and seafood at The Coachman in Hemingway; barbecue in Kingstree and Stuckey at Brown's and Scott's; and chicken bog at Wayne's Pool Hall in Conway. The *National Enquirer* once published an article claiming calories were transmitted across the air. So much for tabloid journalism. If that report were true, I would have weighed three hundred pounds because at one time or another, my nose was under every good cook's pot in the Pee Dee.

The food and scenery of the Pee Dee are certainly exceptional, but it's the people who pop. Take Rossie Bell, long gone, a wino who taught me good character is everything. He'd asked to buy a white bedspread at a garage sale in downtown Hemingway when I was nine. He didn't have the money so he took a day job, promising to return. A smooth-talking woman showed up at lunch, said Rossie wouldn't be back. She wanted the spread. I took her money and sold Rossie's trust for two dollars.

When he returned to learn of my deed, Rossie was furious. "Your mama and grandmama wouldn't have done me that way," he said. "If you're going to be a good woman, you need to keep your promises like them."

I was devastated, but Rossie was right. And I've never forgotten that hard lesson.

When I see Rossie in Heaven, I hope he'll know it, too.

Rossie often helped Daddy, who owned a farm supply warehouse, load fertilizer onto farm trucks. Then on weekends Daddy would wake me up, take me to the bus station in Hemingway for breakfast, and cruise the secondary roads checking on his customers' crops. Mostly his focus was on rain: how much this farmer needed for full Silver Queen or Better Boys, how much would contribute to an early tobacco harvest for the next, or ensure fuller speckled butter beans for yet another.

As we traveled those back roads, all four windows open, Daddy emitted aromas of fertilizer, tobacco, Old Spice and sweat. They were planted so deeply in his skin that Zest couldn't dissolve them. Pee Dee perfume, for sure.

Daddy was the best company ever, no matter where we were—even in church, where narcolepsy often overpowered him. But he was at his finest cruising the back roads of the Pee Dee—to Salters and Gourdin, Prospect and Cades, Andrews and Centenary. Even now when I drive those roads, I feel Dad's presence in the front seat, begging me to pull over for a closer look at Mr. Poston's new John Deere on the Andrews side of Hemingway, or some boiled peanuts at Cooper's Country Store near Salters.

My husband, who hails from Long Island, New York, sampled his first—and last—boiled peanuts at Cooper's. As he popped open a shell, tossed the peanuts onto his tongue and chewed, his face contorted into the most wretched grimace I've ever seen. "I can't taste the excitement," he said. He says the land is beautiful and the people are friendly, but his palate will never be tempted by the collard greens and country ham biscuits at The Coffee Shop in Loris.

I've noticed lately fewer tobacco barns and more empty storefronts in small Pee Dee towns. And I read more about drug busts and factory closings too. But I'm optimistic that the best days for the Pee Dee lie ahead. A Boeing supplier will stumble upon this lost treasure one day. Or perhaps organic farming will revive the farmer's assurance of good fortune.

The region remains open to romance. The essence of the Pee Dee still dwells in all who love the curve of the road, Coca-Cola colored water, historic towns, and the flat, black land. No mountain, no red clay, no ocean will displace the Pee Dee in my heart. ☽

Vennie Deas Moore

)

Mama's House

My mother approaches to relax in the chair behind me. Her hair is silver, but her build and stamina are that of a person years younger. My sons love to visit their grandmother in the village of McClellanville—our family home for generations—despite the abundance of mosquitoes and horseflies almost large enough to ride.

My hometown is a small hamlet along the coast of South Carolina, called the coastal wetlands, which begins just north of Georgetown and runs south to the Florida border. This stretch of coast is separated from the mainland by marshes, alluvial streams, and rivers. Since the marshlands are separated from the coast by tidal estuaries, they have not been accessible until fairly recently except by boat and hand-propelled ferry.

Before the bridges and highways were built and paved in the 1920s and '30s, a trip from Georgetown to McClellanville, twenty miles apart, involved three ferry rides—across the South Santee River, the Santee's North Fork, and the Sampit River. The narrow dirt roads across the river that led to our humble dwelling were only slightly above sea level. During the rainy periods, the roads were inundated and impassable.

The isolation of this village and its small black community of slave descendants meant the influence of the urban white culture was minimal well into the 1940s. Even in the modern era, many dietary, medical, and cultural practices can be traced to African ancestors who had to adapt their ways of life to slavery and a strange environment. Gullah, a Creole language still heard along the coast, was part African, part French, and part seventeenth-century English. "The Old People," as they are called today, brought with them their knowledge of rice growing, basket weaving, fishing, and healing as well as their musical traditions and spiritual beliefs.

Our family, until the 1960s, was self-sufficient. Mama had a vegetable garden and farm animals—goats, hogs, and chickens—and one cow and one mule. Behind our house was nothing but woods. Years ago, the rice fields were up to the ditch, where the old farmers hoed the ditches, plowed the fields, and rolled flat log boats across the river. My daddy and brothers trapped small game, hunted deer, wild ducks, rice birds, and the snapping turtles we called cooters. There were also animals we did not want to confront. Along the ditch, we would walk up on water moccasins and wild hogs.

We lived in a white clapboard shotgun house in the middle of the yard. It had a large screened-in porch and a straight hallway from the front door to the back. Behind the gable windows was a hidden floor, and it had a secret door, too. It was like a dollhouse, offering childhood adventures.

Along the side of our house was a tall bush that looked like a large weed. It was Mullen Leaf; Mama used it for Grandma Mulsie's rheumatism. The Spanish moss hanging from our old oak tree had its uses too. Grandma put it in her shoes to bring down her blood pressure.

Our house during the deep winter months was always cold. About the only warm spot was in front of the open hearth chimney. I always placed my chair too close, and felt like a roasted hen when my mama tossed wood in it and drowned it with kerosene from a steel jug.

We did not have television, and I do not remember listening to the radio. Mama's stories were our entertainment. She told us about Br'er Rabbit, or as she would say, "Bur" Rabbit. Mama grew up hearing these stories. She told them to teach us right from wrong. She would giggle almost throughout the story.

"One day Bur Rabbit decided he would eat the cabbage out of the man's vegetable garden," Mama would tell us. "Just as he started eating, the man came out of his house and caught Bur Rabbit stealing his cabbage. He snuck up behind Bur Rabbit, pulled him up by his ears. The man told Bur Rabbit he was going to throw him in the fire in the yard. Bur Rabbit said, 'Go ahead and throw me in the fire. I would just jump out and run down the road.' The man then said, 'I'll throw you in that briar patch.' Bur Rabbit said, 'Please do not throw me in that briar patch. It would stick me; please do not throw me in the briar patch.' The man by the ear tossed Bur Rabbit in the briar patch. Bur Rabbit got up from being tossed in the briar patch. He looked back at the man as he ran away. Bur Rabbit was laughing: 'You fool! I was born and live in the Briar Patch.'"

Mama's Yard

Just about everything happened in our yard. It was sandy, with patches of tall grass where we did not play. In the cool of the evening, Mama would rake it with crisscross lines to detect grass snakes slithering across the ground. Sulfur was spread to keep those snakes from coming close to the children.

Hogs slopped in the back yard, and there were chicken coops too. Around Easter, we got a litter of brown bunnies. I don't remember the rabbits lasting to the next Easter.

Walking through the yard one day, I came head-on with a Red Head Rooster. He attacked me like a gamecock, leaving both my legs bleeding. Later, after putting iodine on my legs, Mama decided to literally wring his neck. He was our Sunday Dinner. Ironically, Mama invited the preacher for dinner that Sunday. Maybe it was a way to forgive that Red Head Rooster, for his aggressions.

Mama had yard cats. They were not allowed in the house, and Mama made certain they stayed in the yard. She always told the story of the tabby that brought a copperhead snake inside and dropped it at her feet. The cat had wounded it. There it lay in the middle of the dining room. Yard cats are meant to catch lizards, scorpions, and snakes, but they are meant to stay outside with them, she believed.

Mama's Kitchen

Live animals always hung out in my mama's kitchen, before they were cooked. In our old washtub, I would poke at an old cooter with a stick, making sure not to get my fingers too close. It surely would snap my finger off with its hook jaws.

Mama's recipe to cook Yellow Belly Cooter: "I put it in bacon grease. Cut off the black toes, then you work it in flour, black pepper and salt, and you put it in a hot frying pan and then you fry it. And then you turn it over on the other side. Let it brown, and then you add water, onions, and cook it until it's done. If you have any breeding eggs, and shell eggs, when the cooter is done you add the eggs to it and cover it and let it simmer. Then you have a stew . . ."

Blue crabs are the other meat my mother boiled alive. Growing up I caught these crabs on a string with chicken guts tied to it. In the early mornings we went under the bridge to catch them. In the kitchen, alive, they were stacked on top of each other in a wooden crate. As Mama pulled them out they would cling to each other for dear life, not knowing they

Eugenia Deas disciplines a yard cat, 2005.
Photograph by Vennie Deas Moore.

were pulling the others to boiling hot water. With the force of my mama, they formed a chain.

My mama always compared our rural community to crabs in a basket, holding each other back. Maybe it was a way of protecting each other from eternal damnation.

Nights

Nights in the country were darker than dark. You could not see your hands in front of your face, except for the night of the full moon. Then you could see all the stars in the sky.

My daddy and his friends would gather around a bonfire they built in an old oil drum. They tossed old rags and wood logs into the fire to smoke out the gnats. It kept them warm as they laughed after a hard day at work. It was man talk so we were not allowed too close, but we could stand close enough to stay warm. In the summer, fireflies buzzed around, lighting the dark yards.

Along with the stars came all the spirits and the boogey man. You would never catch me walking that country road at night. I am told you would meet up with a ghost dog escaping back to the cemetery.

Daddy painted the window and door trim indigo blue to stop haints from coming through the windows. Some folks call these spooks "plat-eye," because they have just one big eye hinging out in front. I hid my head under my bed cover so I wouldn't see plat eyes in the dark. Mama spread salt outside the doors to keep the hags from riding us at night. The salt would burn the skin the hags shed at night. Hags are female and can assume other forms. They can penetrate a house through the smallest cracks. They can follow you to bed.

Return to Mama's Yard

In the McClellanville I grew up in, blacks and whites were separated and yet connected. There were no fences to keep us in or others out. The closest thing we had to a fence was the chicken wire Mama strung along wooden poles in the front yard. She attached rose bushes to the wire, and honeysuckle vines wrapped around it in the summer. Backyard paths meandered throughout the neighborhood, and everybody was family. In that McClellanville, there was a closeness. The outside world did not matter that much.

About five years ago, we got new neighbors. They moved from someplace in North Carolina. They literally moved into Mama's back yard near the creek. They did not know the ways of the community. The first thing they did after plowing a dirt road to their property was put in a heavy locked cow fence.

Mama had long abandoned that land; she said it was haunted. She had even planted garlic along the edges to protect our yard from the wandering spirits at night. But the new neighbors did not know about those spirits, and Mama didn't tell them any different.

Not long after that, they abandoned the land and moved back to North Carolina. We never understood why they left so suddenly. But Mama said she knew. It was Aunt Hannah. Aunt Hannah didn't give those neighbors a moment of peace, although she died some fifty years ago. ☽

☾

Backyard Bliss

I was born in 1924 on a potato farm in northern Maine close to the Canadian border. Following college and university days, I have lived and worked in Bangor, Maine; Charlottesville and Williamsburg, Virginia; Washington, D.C.; New York City; and Sydney, Australia. However, since 1985 I have resided in Columbia and traveled widely throughout South Carolina, having at some point explored every county. Thus, if asked to name my favorite spot, I undoubtedly would be tempted by the mountain landscape and rolling upland plains, as well as charming vistas found along rivers, lakes, and the Atlantic coast. However, in June 2008 I somehow crossed swords with a freight train stalled near my house and lost . . . lost, in fact, part of my right leg.

This unexpected life twist has not only altered my everyday routine, it has also influenced the selection that follows. Without any reservations whatsoever, top honors would be awarded to my Columbia backyard, a rather undistinguished rectangle stretching from the rear of my Harden Street home west to Waccamaw Street. How big is it? This is only a guess, but I'd say about sixty by eighty feet.

This bit of property certainly is not a manicured delight, but it does include a towering elm, a pecan tree, a large magnolia, a couple of crape myrtles, smaller bushes that may or may not blossom each year, and assorted patches of both lawn grass and plain dirt. It is also home to several extremely active gray squirrels and numerous birds—everything from woodpeckers, bluebirds, doves, wrens, finches, and sparrows to an occasional hummingbird. To the horror of these winged folk, a neighbor's white cat with yellow markings occasionally strolls through the area looking, I presume, for food.

John Hammond Moore observes backyard activity from his kitchen window.
Photograph by Tracy Fredrychowski

Harden Street is widely recognized as the eastern boundary of the original township destined to be our state capital. Less well known is the small subdivision created in 1913, which in effect gave birth to my back yard. Wales Garden, named for banker Edwin Wales Robertson, was an attempt to promote more extensive construction than was taking shape in a growing suburban area east of Harden, a community I can view from my front door. Despite this effort, the entire region—with a wave of the hand—is usually referred to as "Shandon." Robertson, it should be noted, often is credited with the creation of Fort Jackson.

Needless to add, whether viewed from a kitchen window or an adjoining porch, my patchwork of backyard landscape is both active and interesting.

But walk out to Waccamaw Street, turn right, stroll a couple of blocks north, turn left on Wheat Street, and you will run smack into a mass of freight cars stalled on a railway crossing. True, several friends have pointed out the fact that my leg was nearly eighty-five years old and perhaps it was time for an update of some sort. Nevertheless, probably no emphasis or underline is necessary: This is my least favorite spot in all of South Carolina. ☽

Photograph courtesy of Clemson University
Libraries Special Collections.

Evening Quiet

I rest in thy bosom, Carolina. Thy earth and thy air around and above me. In my own country, among my own, I sleep.

Epitaph on the grave of Ben Robertson (1903–1943), journalist, novelist, and author of *Red Hills and Cotton: An Upcountry Memory*

My Own Place

The front porch has always been one of my favorite places. My very presence there transforms it into my own place. It's a restful place to think of the past and enjoy the present surroundings—the smell of freshly cut grass, the beauty of the results of long hours of work planting and weeding flower beds. So often the events and activities of one's childhood shape the very habits we keep as adults.

As far back as I can remember, our front porch played an important role in our daily lives. It was a meeting place, where visitors delivered news good and bad, where neighbors gathered to visit or simply stopped to greet one another.

The front porch of my childhood isn't far from the front porch of my adulthood. Filbert is a small, farming community in rural York County where my family has been since 1915. Generations of my family have lived and farmed peaches and produce, and I've been doing the same since I was a child. My father, a rural elementary school principal back in the days of the Three Rs, started our farm as a single young man. So Filbert has and will always be my home, and even though my houses have changed, their front porches are still where I find refuge.

The front porch of my childhood had sturdy wooden swings and rocking chairs that survived the rain, thunderstorms, ice storms and snow. The smooth, clean-swept hard earth was an ideal front yard for endless games of hopscotch, jump rope, Kick the Can, and No Bears Out Tonight. The front porch was the tag base for competitive running races to and from the mailbox on the main dirt country road.

My special place on that front porch was my very own reading corner. A small wooden bench held my books. It was quite a grand stash. We were a reading family, and we had books, books, books in our home. Because Julius Rosenwald made books available to the schools, we could read all the classics and works of history. Most of my nightly reading was done by kerosene lantern or lamplight, but the best reading was done in the sunlight.

When I was young, my father read to us from *The Sisters,* by James Joyce. I can quote a passage still: "He surely wouldn't survive this time, it was after all his third stroke. Night after night I'd passed the house [it was vacation time] and night after night I studied the lighted square of window, and found it lighted in the same way . . . faintly and evenly."

I always wondered how light could be even. It was never even from the kerosene lamp's wick and surely not from the flicker of a burning candle. It would be years later, when we finally got electricity, that I would realize what even light was all about.

Season after season the front porch set the stage for watching our landscape change. The fresh spring air brought the twitter of returning birds and insects and the beautiful thrust of yellow from blooming shrubs and daffodils. Summer meant the indescribable smell of freshly plowed fields and the occasional glimpse of fleeing deer.

Then there was fall, ushering in its cool crisp air and parade of breathtaking colorful leaves, followed by the winter beauty of icicles dangling, corner to corner, from the porch's wood-shingled roof. They were our popsicles.

I had already settled into my own home, with a much smaller porch, when the old family home burned to the ground. My porch is my writing cottage. It gives me a reprieve from the cleaning and cooking that awaits me inside.

When it comes to happy times, my current porch pales next to the one of my childhood. But then one must remember childhood is best understood or interpreted from the distance of years. Maybe front porches are like Tolstoy's happy families—same in their own way.

Down to this day I still make my way there, mostly during the summer months. The cool shaded areas offer a refreshing retreat from a long day's work in the hot fields or my family's open-air roadside peach stand. From the front porch, the lay of the land stretches out to peach orchards and fields of corn, wheat, and hay.

My mind flows back to the days when the fields were dotted with farmhouses and acres of cotton—cotton everywhere. Stored memories of long past evenings come back, when after days of hard work in the blistering sun tired farmers gathered for a few restful hours in the late evening shade to sing

The view from Dori Sanders' front porch in Filbert.
Photograph by Katherine Lemon Stoyer.

soulful songs. Their singing pealed across the countryside, often blending with other farmers playing mournful tunes on homemade harmonicas or out-of-tune guitars, belting out the blues they made up as they went along.

For fleeting moments, the memories and sounds all rush in. I can hear them all, or so it seems. Nearly always there is that still, quiet space of time as the dusk gently fades into darkness—that small frame of hushed time before the insects and tree frogs begin their nightly symphony.

I cradle a glass of sweet iced tea, savor its delicious taste, and listen to the quiet. ☽

CONTRIBUTORS

A lifelong resident of the Carolina lowcountry, WILLIAM P. BALDWIN is an award-winning novelist, poet, biographer, and historian. He graduated from Clemson University with a B.A. in history and an M.A. in English. For nine years he ran a shrimp boat and then built houses, but the principal occupation of his life has been writing. He enjoys kayaking, and one of these days he absolutely, definitely will make the paddle from the mainland to Bulls Island and back.

Lancaster native KENDALL BELL is an award-winning journalist, author, and speaker whose newspaper career spanned more than twenty years. His latest book is *Larry Phillips: NASCAR's Only Five-Time Winston Racing Series Champion*. He lives in Sumter, where he's at work on a mystery series.

CYNTHIA BOITER is the author of *Buttered Biscuits: Short Stories from the South* and the editor of *Jasper Magazine*. She is a six-time winner of the South Carolina Fiction Project, a three-time winner of the Piccolo Fiction Open, a winner of the Porter Fleming Award for fiction, and a former fellow with the South Carolina Academy of Authors for creative nonfiction. She is a member of the adjunct faculty at the University of South Carolina, where she teaches women's and gender studies.

SHANE BRADLEY is the author of two books, *Mourning Light* and *The Power and the Glory*, and a two-time winner of the South Carolina Fiction Project. He lives in Due West, where he teaches high school English and is adjunct professor of English at Anderson University.

LEE GORDON BROCKINGTON is the author of three books, including *Plantation Between the Waters: A Brief History of Hobcaw Barony*. She is senior interpreter at Hobcaw Barony in Georgetown County.

Allendale native KEN BURGER spent forty years covering sports, business, and people for two South Carolina newspapers and was named one of the country's best sports columnists three times. His columns for the Charleston *Post and Courier* have been collected in *Baptized in Sweet Tea*; his trilogy of South Carolina fiction includes *Swallow Savannah, Sister Santee,* and *Salkehatchie Soup.* Burger graduated dead last in his class at the University of Georgia, has been married five times, and is a cancer survivor.

AMANDA CAPPS is an award-winning journalist who helps aspiring writers polish and market their work. Her long-term goals include winning a hot-dog-eating contest at Just Dogs while maintaining a weight of less than 135 pounds. The author/competitive eater lives in Greenville.

JOHN CELY is a lifelong resident of Columbia and former land-protection director for the Congaree Land Trust. He retired from the South Carolina Department of Natural Resources after twenty-six years as a wildlife biologist. He is the author of *Cowassee Basin: The Green Heart of South Carolina.* His involvement with the Congaree National Park, which includes long-term bird studies and searching for champion trees, goes back nearly forty years.

PAT CONROY is the author of several novels, including *The Prince of Tides, Beach Music, The Water Is Wide,* and *The Great Santini.* He also has written a cookbook and a memoir about his years playing basketball.

Charleston native ROBIN ASBURY CUTLER lives and writes in Franklin, Tennessee. She formerly worked for Amazon.com, the University of Wisconsin, Newberry College, and the University of South Carolina, and she was publisher of Summerhouse Press in Columbia. Cutler continues to support the work of Connie Maxwell Children's Home. Though the library and church she remembers so well were torn down years ago, the White-Morehead Cottage still houses children in a family-style setting.

BILLY DEAL is a former sports editor for the *Savannah Morning News* and freelance sports journalist. In 2009 he published *Sports Legends: 50 Years of Photographs and Memories.* He lives in Columbia.

CLAIR DELUNE is a Columbia media/public relations professional and writer as well as a music historian, professor, and host of *Blues Moon Radio,* one of the longest-running roots music radio shows in the country.

NATHALIE DUPREE is the author of twelve books and host of more than 300 television episodes airing on PBS, TLC, and the Food Network. A Charleston resident, she writes for local and other papers and magazines.

Hemingway native **MARY EADDY** is the author of *The Oaks of McCord*. She lives along the Grand Strand.

STARKEY FLYTHE'S latest collection of fiction is *Driving with Hand Controls*. The former managing editor of *Holiday* and *Saturday Evening Post*, Flythe lives in North Augusta, his hometown.

Lexington native **DANIEL ELTON HARMON** is the author of more than seventy grade-level educational books and is a veteran magazine, newsletter, and newspaper editor and writer. He also writes short mystery fiction set in late-nineteenth-century South Carolina. He lives in Spartanburg.

STEPHEN G. HOFFIUS is a freelance writer and editor in Charleston. Among his recent books are *Upheaval in Charleston: Earthquake and Murder on the Eve of Jim Crow* (with Susan Millar Williams) and *The Life and Art of Alfred Hutty: Woodstock to Charleston* (with Sara C. Arnold).

Columbia native **CECILE S. HOLMES** is the former religion editor of the *Houston Chronicle*, where she was nominated seven times for the Pulitzer Prize. The author of *Four Women, Three Faiths*, Holmes is at work on a third book about the spirituality of World War II servicemen and -women. She is associate professor of journalism and mass communications at the University of South Carolina.

DOT JACKSON is a former newspaper writer who worked for years with one beat in mind—the Keowee Bureau. Her aim was to sit by the river and report when a kingfisher made a catch or a laurel bloom floated by. Instead she wrote *Refuge*, an award-winning novel set in Pickens County, where she now lives at the foot of Table Rock. Jackson is director of the Birchwood Center for Arts and Folklife.

DIANNE JOHNSON is a professor of English at the University of South Carolina. As Dinah Johnson, she is the author of a number of children's books, including *All Around Town: The Photographs of Richard Samuel Roberts, Hair Dance*, and *Black Magic*. Her daughter, Niani Feelings, is the light of her life.

SANDRA JOHNSON is the author of *Standing on Holy Ground: A Triumph Over Hate Crime in the Deep South*, for which she won a Christopher Award for literature. A Columbia native, she is an adjunct professor at University of South Carolina–Sumter and Midlands Technical College. She is currently at work on a novel set in the lowcountry of South Carolina.

JOHN LANE is an associate professor of English and environmental studies at Wofford College in Spartanburg and director of the college's Goodall Environmental Studies Center. He is the author of a dozen books of poetry and prose. The latest are *Abandoned Quarry: New and Selected Poems, My Paddle to the Sea*, and a new essay collection, *Begin with Rock, End with Water*.

J. DREW LANHAM is a native of Edgefield and a professor of Wildlife Ecology at Clemson University. His writings about home and land ethic, naturalist William Bartram, deer hunting, and the struggles between race and self-identity in travels abroad have appeared in various anthologies. His first solo work, *The Home Place: Memoirs of a Colored Man's Love Affair with Nature*, recently was published by Milkweed Editions.

NICK LINDSAY is a former professor, poet, carpenter, and boat builder who lives on Edisto Island. His book, *And I'm Glad: An Oral History of Edisto Island*, recalls the island through the voices of its natives. Lindsay worked as a carpenter at the Savannah River Site from 1951 through 1954.

McClellanville native VENNIE DEAS MOORE is a folklorist and photographer in Columbia. Her books include *Home: Portraits from the Carolina Coast* and *Scenes from Columbia's Riverbanks: A History of the Waterways*.

JOHN HAMMOND MOORE has been a news reporter, book editor, and history teacher in South Carolina, Georgia, and Australia. A World War II Navy veteran, he has published more than twenty books, the latest titled *Carnival of Blood: Dueling, Lynching, and Murder in South Carolina, 1880–1920*. He lives in Columbia.

SAM MORTON is a writer and novelist in Columbia. During his Citadel career, he earned the Mark Clark Award, the highest award given to a Citadel summer camper, and the President's Award for Creative Youth Development, the highest honor bestowed on a camp counselor. As a senior cadet officer, he was named social chair and was presented the David S. McAlister Student Activities Award just before graduation. He is a life member of the Citadel Alumni Association.

Hollywood native HORACE MUNGIN studied English at Fordham University. His poetry and prose have been published in many publications, including the *New York Times* and *Essence Magazine*. He has six books to his credit.

KIRK H. NEELY is senior pastor of Morningside Baptist Church in Spartanburg and the author of eight books. He and his wife, Clare, are native South Carolinians who have lived in Spartanburg since 1980.

LIZ NEWALL'S features, fiction, and poetry have appeared in publications across the country. She is a four-time winner in the S.C. Fiction Project, and her novel, *Why Sarah Ran Away with the Veterinarian*, was endorsed by Lee Smith and selected among the state's top fiction the year it was released. A native of upstate South

Carolina, she wrote for *Clemson World* magazine for more than two decades and edited it for seventeen years.

TOM POLAND has published six books, three with photographer Robert C. Clark. *Reflections of South Carolina, Volume II* is their fourth photo-essay book to be published by the University of South Carolina Press. Poland's "Across The Savannah" columns reflect a changing South. Swamp Gravy, Georgia's Folk Life Drama, produced his play *Solid Ground.* A native of Lincolnton, Georgia, and a graduate of the University of Georgia, he lives in Columbia.

AÏDA ROGERS is a writer and editor in Columbia. She and Tim Driggers are coauthors of *Stop Where the Parking Lot's Full,* a guidebook to South Carolina's favorite restaurants.

DORI SANDERS is a farmer and the author of *Clover, Her Own Place, Dori Sanders' Country Cooking: Recipes and Stories from the Family Farm Stand,* and *Promise Land: A Farmer Remembers.* She lives in her home community of Filbert, in York County.

W. THOMAS SMITH JR. is director of the U.S. Counterterrorism Advisory Team and former U.S. Marine rifle-squad leader. He writes about military/defense issues and has covered conflict in the Balkans, on the West Bank, in Iraq, and in Lebanon. The author of six books, Smith is a *New York Times* best-selling military technical adviser and editor. He lives in Columbia.

DENO TRAKAS is a poet, fiction writer, professor, and chair of the Department of English at Wofford College in Spartanburg. His most recent book is *Because Memory Isn't Eternal: A Story of Greeks in Upstate South Carolina.*

Moncks Corner native **CEILLE BAIRD WELCH** is an award-winning playwright. Two of her favorites, *The Very First Milo Moose Day Celebration* and *A Rainbow of a Different Color,* are musicals for children. She lives with her husband, Jim, on a rambling homestead in Hopkins, South Carolina, and in a log cabin at Pinnacle Falls near Flat Rock, North Carolina.

MARJORY WENTWORTH'S poems have been nominated for the Pushcart Prize five times. Her books of poetry include *Noticing Eden, Despite Gravity, The Endless Repetition of an Ordinary Miracle,* and *What the Water Gives Me.* She also is the author of *Shackles,* an award-winning children's book. She teaches at the Art Institute of Charleston and Roper St. Francis Hospital and is the Poet Laureate of South Carolina.